THE RELUCTANT

THE RELUCTANT PSYCHIC

DYAN GRANT-FRANCIS

HORSDAL & SCHUBART

Horsdal & Schubart Publishers Ltd.
Victoria, BC, Canada

Cover: Photograph by Gregg Eligh, Victoria, BC.

Photographs are by the author unless otherwise credited.

This book is set in Bitstream Arrus.

We acknowledge the support of the Canada Council for the Arts for our publishing program.
We also acknowledge the assistance of the Province of British Columbia, through the British Columbia Arts Council.

Printed and bound in Canada by Printcrafters, Winnipeg, Manitoba.

Canadian Cataloguing in Publication Data

Grant-Francis, Dyan, 1948-
The reluctant psychic

Includes bibliographical references.
ISBN 0-920663-65-6

1. Grant-Francis, Dyan, 1948-. 2. Psychics—Canada—Biography. I. Title.

BF1027.G73A3 1999   133.8'092   C99-910274-5

Printed and bound in Canada

"The most beautiful and profound emotion we can experience is the sensation of the mystical. It is the sower of all true science. He to whom this emotion is a stranger, who can no longer wonder and stand rapt in awe, is as good as dead."

Albert Einstein

CONTENTS

Acknowledgments

As I REFLECT on the genesis of this book, I feel awed and blessed by the many people who journeyed with me, always willing to help and give support in whatever way was needed. I would like to use this space to send a gentle breeze of thanks to all who participated in some way, and acknowledge the following for kindness above and beyond the call of duty, as my father would say:

My sister of the heart, Jane Smith, for 46 years of steadfast and caring friendship;

Karen Sihota — friend, confidante and wise woman, who shone light into the dark places;

Penny Briggs, who patiently listened to my struggle in birthing the first draft of this book;

My friend Doug Ellis, for his willingness to encourage my halting steps into the world of commas, quotes and storytelling;

My sons — Devin with the energy of poetry and gentleness and Aiden with the energy of fire and compassion, who patiently understood my hours at the computer;

Beth Hill, who would scold me for the tears in my eyes as I write of my feeling of deep gratitude for the privilege of knowing her and her family;

Bruce Ihara, whose sureness with acupuncture needles guided me through my health challenges to increased vision and clarity;

Sandra Fisher of the Psychic Circle, who believed in me enough to give me encouragement and my first real job as a psychic reader, and who stayed in touch despite crazy schedules;

Laurice Mock, whose wisdom and amazing psychic gifts guided me through these uncharted waters;

Phoenix, my sister from ancient times, for bringing palm trees, laughter and heartfelt sanctuary unconditionally;

Linda and Jack, my soul mates, who offered me a home when I had no other, and their malamute, Sheba, who lay across the bedroom doorway, reminding me to stay at my computer and write, instead of going to the lake to dream;

Marlyn Horsdal, my editor and publisher, for her curiosity about and belief in the possibility of a psychic realm;

Rick Ellis, forever and always my greatest love and, in the end, my greatest teacher;

And last but definitely not least, my eternal thankfulness for Spirit, my guiding light on this Earth journey, the power that calls me forward, always challenging me to get out of my comfort zone and explore new worlds;

And a huge thank you to my clients, my students and everyone else I haven't named specifically.

Bright Blessings,
Dyan

CHAPTER ONE

EMERGENCE

PSYCHIC CONNECTIONS

IT WAS ONE of "those" days when you could feel the energy of change in the air. It was filled with weak winter sun, a watery cool January light that poured through the panes of my kitchen window into the sink just below, bringing rainbows to the soapy bubbles that covered the breakfast dishes. Staring into the ferns of frost growing up from the window sill, I was trying to figure out how to find a job.

Scanning the Victoria papers day after day looking for work, I found there were no advertisements that matched the skills I had developed through many years with the government and none that caught my interest. I felt at the end of my rope, puzzled and confused about where to look next, ready to apply for any job that was available. Tracing the lines of a freshly washed plate, I realized that the patterns of my day were as frozen and set as the ice on the windowpane in front of me.

1

"Oh, well," I thought, hearing my mother's voice, "when things get this stuck something's got to change!" Carrying my coffee cup over to the table I joined my teenaged son in reading the morning newspaper, the classifieds of course. "Ah, the predictable texture of my days," I mused.

Then I saw the ad, glowing as if under a spotlight, calling my attention. "ARE YOU A PSYCHIC, AN ASTROLOGER, A CARD READER? WE'RE LOOKING FOR PEOPLE INTERESTED IN WORKING IN THESE AREAS." A phone number was given.

I thought, "Oh no, I'm not ready for this." I can't read cards and I know very little about astrology. Psychic? I'd tried to avoid that label for most of my life. And yet, this ad was definitely calling to me, this life I'd tried to deny for years. It shone there in the paper like a beacon, a lighthouse marking the safe passage.

Yet it didn't feel safe to me. In my growing years I'd been called "too sensitive," "over imaginative" and "crazy" often enough to cause me to believe those labels. Looking out the window into the white wintry world beyond, so still and hushed, I wondered if I dared risk the leap of faith that would cause me to challenge those long-held beliefs and the fear underlying them.

For a few moments I watched a flock of birds perched at the feeder, finding seed through the snow, their feathers fluffed up in the cold air. The family sounds of a Saturday morning, coffee percolating, spoons against cereal bowls, receded into the background.

Without another thought I walked over to the phone and then stopped and turned away, letting my fear control my feet. I sat back down ... and then got up and reached for the phone again. I dialed the number and promptly heard the phone ring on the other end.

I learned that day that the first step off the cliff when you're learning to fly is definitely the hardest — and the smallest.

A man answered, "Psychic Line, can I help you?"

My stomach was flying up into my throat, trying to seal up my voice, before I said; "Yes, I saw your ad about looking for psychics."

"Just a moment." Oh no, don't give me an opportunity to hang up now.

A second voice answered, more cheerful than the first, "Hi, can I help you?" Without giving in to my trembling knees and sweating palms, I told her the reason for my call. She asked if I was psychic.

"Well, some people think I am, but I don't really know," was my hesitant reply.

"Do you read cards or anything?" she asked.

"No, I don't."

"Well, why don't you do a reading of me right now?"

"Now?!" came my horrified voice. I had no idea what to do. "Wing it" came the prompting thought — from somewhere.

"Sure, now," she said in a southern drawl. "Don't be nervous."

"Well, okay, I'll give it a shot," thinking all the while, "Oh, yeah, easy for you to say."

"Do you need me to tell you anything?"

"No," I said. "I don't."

"Whoa!" my mind shrieked. "Wait a minute! Do you really know what you're doing?" And with that I closed my eyes, took a very deep breath, said a quick prayer for help and began to tell Nancy what I could pick up about her.

"Well, I have a sense that you've just left your partner and you're feeling very confused about whether that was the right decision. It seems you felt very limited by this man, and yet cared for him deeply. He seems to have been very busy with his work, or maybe it was a hobby, with not much time for you, and yet he wanted you to stay at home waiting for him."

And then the pictures in my mind's eye started to flow, and I began to speak about them.

"A white car was used in the move. Your new apartment has a great view from the bedroom but you're not sleeping well at night. It seems that your mom is sick and you're worried about her. You're also concerned about your health and how you're going to manage everything, but it looks like your mom is okay, and that all the bills do get paid. Do you have a white car?" I finally stopped and asked. I also remembered to breathe at that

3

point. I wondered, as I had for many years, where all this information came from, and how did I know it?

"No, I don't, but he does," came the reply. "That's exactly right. I'm so confused and I don't know what to do! Boy, are you ever good. How about working for us?"

Astonished would be too small a word to describe all that I was feeling.

There it was; the call to fly into a new future and turn the obstacles of my past, the things I had tried so desperately to avoid and deny, into the building blocks of a new life. And especially a new job!

I slowly felt my awareness return to the kitchen. I was somehow surprised that it was still there, my warm coffee cup sitting on the table. It was a very strange feeling, to know that I had seen into Nancy's life while she was sitting at a desk in Florida, and then to see my son still eating his breakfast as if nothing had happened. "Earth-shattering events" are often lost on teenagers with food.

"I have a job," I announced.

He looked up in disbelief. "Doing what?" he asked.

"Doing psychic readings on a 900 line."

His single raised eyebrow said it all.

I went around the house in disbelief that day, disbelief mixed with excitement; a curious sense of being far removed from the world as it was yesterday. The snow was still on the ground, the birds digging away for the seed in the feeder, yet my experience of the world had changed to one that was less limited, less restricted in some sense, with much more freedom. Pizza and a movie capped the celebration of my new job.

The front door shut quickly as my son came in out of the cold the next Monday.

"Guess what, Mom! I told everybody about your new job."

"How did they respond?" I inquired.

"Well ..." He started to describe how his friends began teasing him that I was really working on a 900 sex line. It fit their image of me as that weird mother who ate strange food and probably grew pot in her bedroom closet. I suspect there is some status in

4

having the strangest mom in the school, although "psychic" may have been a little too strange for those conservative, private-school students.

As I filled out the forms for employment with the Psychic Line, I kept trying to convince myself that I had made the right decision, as if there were any other choice. It was time to move fully into who I was and there was no going back. I realized it was like becoming pregnant; once it's done, the change is permanent.

***

I never consciously wanted to be psychic. It just seemed so natural and such a part of me that I didn't really notice it or think about what I "knew" as anything to do with psychic abilities. However, I did learn, as a child, to keep quiet about the things I knew. I've been curious about psychic phenomena off and on throughout my life, intrigued by things like ESP, telepathy and mystical occurrences. While I discounted my own psychic awareness as "imagination," "luck," or "just a hunch," the more I studied the ideas of metaphysics and shamanism, and the psychic skills of remote viewing and intuitive medicine, the more I could see parallels between these and my own experiences.

I invite you along on my journey of exploration, seeking to bridge science and metaphysics, to harmonize seemingly opposing world views into rational ways of perceiving our world and all it encompasses. I have no explanation of "how" my psychic ability works, but the "why" is partly answered by my intense curiosity about the psychic way of being, and my quest to find answers and insight into what this means for me, for humanity and for our planet.

Come and share these stories of awakening, these direct experiences of embracing the psychic world and the subtle energies that flow through it.

CHAPTER TWO

AWAKENING

BLUEBELLS AND FAIRY RINGS

I WONDERED, AS a child, how and why I "knew" things and what was supposed to be done with the knowledge. Sometimes it was fun to fool the adults when I knew something that I had no ordinary way of knowing but other times it was distressing and unwelcome.

The earliest memories I have of knowing relate to knowing that everything is alive — the plants, lightning, thunder, stones. Though this certainly reflected a child's active imagination, I also had a deep and certain knowing.

I remember arguing with my mother when I was four that all the rocks in my bedroom were alive with beings that were my friends. Just after this argument I was taken to hospital with double pneumonia and spent many weeks in an oxygen tent fighting for my life. I longed for the rocks and plants to keep me company in that sterile environment.

It's the bluebells I remember the most, from the spring days of my childhood. Tender plants never seen in florist shops, they grew in profusion in the hidden space beside our house. Between the two houses, that of my parents and our next-door neighbors, was a narrow space about eight feet wide that stretched for the length of the houses. It was hidden by dense plantings of trees and bushes at either end; my best friend Karen and I had made it our secret hideout. We would disappear through that wall of trees and be out of sight in a flash, transported into our own magical land.

The winters in Vancouver held the soggy, grey dampness of the rainclouds that sat, day after day, at the feet of the Coast Mountains, making our hidden land too wet for play. Those first green shoots emerging from the wet winter soil would bring us a sense of anticipation for the approaching spring. As the earth dried, the bluebells grew and our hidden spot was filled with sunshine again.

It was in that space that I first met the fairies, those tiny spirits that looked after the trees and the land. The bluebells would herald their arrival.

With hushed voices we would move between the bushes each day to see if they had come. There was a lightness that filled the space; a tingling that could be sensed. It felt like instant excitement. I don't remember when we first noticed them, but it seemed they had always been there, with the springtime.

Their presence was so normal in those days that we never questioned it. They were just a unique feature of our already special spot and we were delighted by them. With their arrival we knew that summer was just around the corner.

Any noise or motion would cause them to disappear but if we were very, very still we could watch them dance on a moss ring that grew in the center of that field of flowers. It was an almost perfect circle of spongy, brilliant emerald, green moss and always clear of leaves and debris even though the rest of the ground could be littered. We would watch them brush and tend the ring, and although they never talked to us directly, we came away filled with a magical sense of caring for the land and the living things that grew there.

They were creatures that, if looked at directly, would disappear. Watching them always meant looking beside them rather than at them, and looking sideways to see the whole area.

I always thought that Karen could see the fairies too, that we shared this awareness, until years later when we reminisced about those times past, and she said she could not. While I was playing with the fairies, she had been playing with me, going along with the game because she was my friend.

This circle of living beings had transported my mundane world of piano practice and homework into the mystery of a landscape where fairies, gnomes and Elementals would come out to play in the stillness. It was in this place, with those guardian spirits that were responsible for caretaking the land, that my young eyes were first opened, albeit briefly.

Perhaps humans stopped seeing the fairies at the time of the Industrial Revolution. With all the noise and clatter of machinery we lost our mystical connection with the land. It took us from the countryside into the factories and then into the boardrooms of concrete and steel buildings with voice mail, cell phones and computers — the modern age.

I can still hear my mother's voice saying, "Shh — they'll hear you." I was never sure if she meant the spirits or the neighbors. Years later, I learned that although Mom could sense other beings, and often intuitively knew what was going to happen, she would not admit to of any of this when I was young. Nor would she talk about her family or her childhood.

One evening when she was older, the unexpected reasons for this came to light. We had gathered together on the occasion of a visit from my elderly Uncle Les. Candles lit the dining-room table, spread with the family silver and her best white linen cloth. Serving dishes holding the remnants of one of Mom's great Olde English roast-beef dinners lay scattered over the cloth like spent offerings. The headlights of cars on Lions Gate Bridge brought a sense of movement to the fixed night lights of Vancouver as I gazed out the windows of her twelfth-story apartment. Questions I wanted to ask of this brother and sister, about their long journey from a small village near Swansea in Wales to the shores of an ocean on the other side of the world, filled my head. They were reminiscing about old times, as seniors are wont to do.

Finally, I thought, after all these years I might get some insight into the psychic past of my family. It turned out to be one of those very sad and tragic stories that you read about in the chronicles of small and small-minded towns.

My grandparents had divorced early in this century, an event almost unheard-of in those times. My grandmother had a "breakdown" as a result of the trauma and was hospitalized. Grandma was eventually released from the asylum where she had been kept for years because she could "see things," a dangerous condition then.

Grandma moved away from the city, as if to escape all that had happened there, to a small town in a valley in Wales. A reclusive, rather eccentric woman, she was sought out by the farmers to heal their animals and help with birthing. She lived quietly for many years, traveling through the valleys, sharing her gifts for healing with any who asked, until there was a murder in the next town. Having dreamed of the murder nights before, Grandma promptly marched off to the police station to tell them what she had seen. However, police don't listen to crazy women, and so the case remained unsolved until years later, when the body was discovered, exactly as Grandma had told them.

While we all have access to "second sight," in some cases it's in the family, and both my parents had a fairly well-developed sense of intuition.

The first confirmation of my knowing occurred one July day when I was eight, with enough drama to frighten me. This was far more than playing games with sweet fairies.

In the warmth of that summer, my friends and I would raid our mothers' closets for the longest, most dramatic scarves and any jewelry that looked like something a fortune-teller would wear. We wandered from house to house, much like the gypsies of old, finding cats to heal and palms to read, and telling each other about the handsome men we would someday marry.

Yet this seemed like more than just a game to be played until we heard the ice cream truck and went running down the street to buy Popsicles. I lived in those gypsy clothes, and had unending ideas about how to embellish this pastime and weave it into endless days of exploration for myself and my friends. Last summer's cowboys and Indians were chased away by gypsy glitter.

We set up a lemonade stand at the bottom of our street for a few days. The kitchen could have been declared a disaster area by the time we finished cutting the lemons and finding the ice. No Koolaid for such adventuresome wanderers. Sitting at the lemonade stand in my gypsy robes, I was transported into another time and would play the part of a wise old woman, peering into the future, while neighbors bought lemonade. Until that day in July when the rules of the game changed dramatically.

"Oh Mr. Brown, I see you ... I see you moving ... soon, very soon [in a deep mysterious voice] to another town so far away. All the boxes, those boxes ... I can see all the boxes in your house. Ooh," [I would do my best imitation of a fortune-teller] "you'll have to leave Blondie behind." Blondie was the family's cocker spaniel and a very spoiled fat little dog.

"Why is that?" Mr. Brown asked, going along with this child's play.

"Because she's going to be too sick to go," I said in a conspiratorial whisper.

"Oh, that would be a shame, but we're not going to be moving. Thanks for the lemonade."

Two weeks later the For Sale sign went up, and by the time the moving trucks came, Blondie had been put to sleep because she was dying from disease in her stomach.

I asked Mom when I saw the For Sale sign, and she told me Mr. Brown had lost his job suddenly and they had to move. I told her about that afternoon at the lemonade stand, and she gave me her usual reply, "Oh, it's all in your imagination."

This game held us mesmerized for the whole summer; over and over we would create gypsy wagons and fortune-telling tents, immersed in tales of magic and silver crossing our palms. While nothing really bad happened that summer, I became less and less willing to share what I knew, for fear that "It" might be wrong, or perhaps, that "It" might actually be right.

THE LEARNING PLACE

Often, answers and teaching come through our dreams. Insightful, accurate and instructive, dreams open the door into inaccessible parts of our psyche. Rich in metaphor, they speak in the language of symbols, of analogy, of paradox. From the stories of Daniel's dreams and visions in the lion's den, through the insights of Carlos Castaneda and Don Juan, Edgar Cayce and Nostradamus, dreams have long been used as tools of prophesy and divination. Jung used them to begin his exploration of the hidden realms of the human unconscious, and dream interpretation has a growing fascination for many people today.

Nightmares and unusual dreams sometimes fill the time of psychic opening, as our minds try to sort out the flood of information that is being received on so many previously unknown levels of consciousness. This happens when our psyches expand and open, when our conscious awareness and physical body have become sensitive to the internal prompting of intuition and to the external energies flowing around us.

Banshees haunted my nights during the gypsy summer. As I lay awake in the dark, shrieking, white, wild-haired specters would fly at me from the top of my closet across the room, over and over, always screaming soundlessly. I longed for sleep, for these images to go away forever. What I did was close my eyes, praying to go to sleep. If I couldn't make these spirits go away, I would just pretend they didn't exist.

Yet my childhood also held other spirits, who were friendlier than the banshees. Three guides first appeared one night the winter when I was nine; three who have stayed with me throughout my life. They came quietly that first night, gently so as not to be frightening. They just sat in my dream and I wondered what they were doing there. They were dark, short and broad, very masculine in their appearance, and hairy.

11

They have worn a variety of garments through the years, sometimes hats, sometimes white robes, yet I always knew them by their eyes, like liquid pools, wide and clear as crystals. The first spirit had eyes of deep, deep brown, the second spirit had aqua eyes like the ocean, and the third had eyes like clear amber. They have never spoken to me, although I always knew what they wanted to tell me. In my literal brain, they truly appeared as guides, leading me to new places and experiences in my dreams. They were the only beings that I would follow unquestioningly.

These dreams are still alive in my memory, with the color and intensity I first experienced, though they occurred several decades ago.

One night, my guides led me into realms far from Earth. One minute I was asleep, the next I was aware of standing in my bedroom, out of my bed, dressed in my nightgown. As they took my hands we moved silently through the walls of my room into the outside world.

"Wow," I thought, with the wonder of childhood acceptance.

Once outside we drifted higher. The air got darker until it felt as though we were moving through some kind of dark hallway. The surrounding space changed from a view of the night lights around my house to a sunny day in a place that had three suns. I remember looking at the sky and counting them over and over until I thought there must be something wrong with my eyes. How could there be three suns? I looked at the trio quizzically, and they smiled.

I noticed grass under my feet and a white building in the distance. It was a peculiar experience; the details of the area surrounding me came slowly, as if I were waking up and noticing one thing at a time, unable to comprehend the complete picture.

As we went along, I saw other people walking toward the building. They looked friendly but seemed unaware of us. When we entered the building I thought, "Oh no, not more school!" It had the appearance of a complex of school classrooms.

The teachers were dressed in white robes and they appeared ancient to my young eyes. This complex was situated in a grassy green field alongside a river and built of gleaming white stone. There were many reflecting pools set in the gardens. My guides led me though the complex as if to say "See where you can go when you graduate." It did seem more like a university than the public school I was in. As we walked on, the people continued to ignore us. They were busy going from room to room and listening in each one. We must have been a peculiar sight though, three dark men and one young girl in a nightgown.

The next morning when I woke up I wondered where I had been. I felt quite safe and rested. I fell asleep the next night thinking about the Learning Place, curious about what was going on there and wanting to go back and explore. I awoke in the dream of the Learning Place, emerging into an empty hallway and as I stood there, the students came up to me and smiled. They gestured for me to go into a classroom and sit down. I was delighted. After all, what nine-year-old doesn't like that kind of attention?

Feeling as though I was on a very daring adventure, I went to the Learning Place often during the next year. The students were always pleased to see me and would sneak me into class. They were joyful people and I thought of them as my friends.

I didn't understand much of what was said at the time; I just listened quietly, trying to absorb as much as I possibly could. It felt so special to be there that I wasn't going to cause trouble. It was so much more interesting than the multiplication tables I was learning in Grade Four!

I can see the wisdom in the teachings now, with subjects like eternal truth, justice, divine love and compassion. These principles provided a vision of a world based on respect, honor and integrity. This was a world where space, time and any concept of separation between things did not seem to exist, and where cause and effect were not linked. This was a world very different from our own physical reality and one that bore many similarities to the psychic realm.

13

The stories told of this sacred way of being were filled with a deep understanding of the uniqueness and interconnection of all life, where planets were seen as single living organisms: where energy was the basis of life and the enhancement of its vibration useful for healing and restoration.

The students there told me that they had lived on Earth at different times. They said that since they had seen the view of life and consciousness from an Earthly perspective, now they were getting the "big picture," the eternal perspective, as they called it, that was appropriate to their stage of development. All the students were in the same grade; as they explained it, this was almost like a debriefing of their experiences on Earth, before the next stage was embarked upon.

Years later, in my explorations of life after death, I came to see more clearly where the Learning Place might fit in the geography and pathway of the next world, the location of "there" after the Bardo, written of in *The Tibetan Book of Living and Dying*.

Although I listened intently to the teachings, I was still unable to understand much of what was said. I remember the teachers saying that Love was all, and pain came from holding on to what wasn't Love. I didn't understand then as I do now.

I visited in their classrooms for almost a year, an unaware little girl who liked to play gypsy. Then, one night, one of the "wise ones," that were the Masters or teachers at the Learning Place, called to me to sit with him beside the river. He explained that this place was for those who had left Earth and were continuing their journey here. He gently told me that I had to stay on Earth for a while, that I needed to complete my learning on Earth. I felt very sad and angry. Though I forgot the pathway back, I never forgot the lessons.

I used to share all my dreams and psychic insights with my dad. He always accepted what I described as accurate pictures of my experience, and encouraged me to explore them for deeper meaning and greater understanding. He was a practising Zen Buddhist, his philosophy strongly reflected in his words and feelings; we talked about my experiences and he shared some of his. It was comforting, yet I remained afraid of what was happening to me.

14

THE OUIJA BOARD

Even in our earliest memories, some of us wonder if there is anything under the bed. Is there something in that dark space, waiting? Something we can't see? We have a sense that the space is not empty.

When Karen and I were young, Ouija boards opened the doorway to the idea of spirits outside our usual world in a more tangible way than the fairies had. Perhaps there was something under that bed!

We had bought a Ouija board during our usual Saturday afternoon shopping excursion. We had unpacked it quietly, not wanting Karen's sisters to hear us, and were sitting on the bed in her room, pillows propped up behind our backs. We set the board, a piece of cardboard covered with numbers and the letters of the alphabet, on the quilt. It came with a plastic, triangle-shaped pointer which would indicate the letter and on which we rested our fingers.

"Let's try it. What do we do?" we whispered.

"Are there any instructions?"

"Let's just put our fingers here and ask a question."

"Who will I marry?"

"Okay, close our eyes. Ready?"

Nothing.

Two teenaged girls sat expectantly, waiting for something to happen that might show them their future.

"Let's try again only this time concentrate harder."

"On what?" Karen asked.

"On the question, I guess. Okay, fingers on, eyes closed."

Nothing!

"Let's try one more time," we agreed.

Fingers on, eyes closed.

"You pushed it."

"No I didn't."

"Yes you did."

"No, really I didn't."

"But it moved!"

"Okay, let's try it again ... but don't push it!"
There was an air of excitement in the room.
"Oh my, did you feel that?"
"It moved," came the whispered reply.
IT MOVED!
We looked at each other in shock. We tried again, it moved again, and spelled out "Bob."
We put the board away in the very, very top of Karen's cupboard, in the darkness at the back of the highest shelf. This was more than either of us could allow into our lives of school and fingernail polish.
However, the doorway into another world had opened a little bit more, although it would be years before we were ready to enter. Neither of us married a Bob but we did date boys called Bob.
We wondered. Was this a ghost speaking through the board, through our fingers? What was the energy that moved the plastic piece and, most importantly, was it friendly? We had all sorts of ideas of disembodied spirits, but we didn't really know.

GO AWAY, WE'RE CLOSED!

As I grew through my teens, I developed a great case of adolescent angst. I felt more and more as though I was a stranger on this planet, that I didn't really belong here, and I didn't like it. I felt frighteningly alone, with nowhere to fit in, nowhere to belong. As a result I tried harder to be "average," "normal," "like everyone else," to find a place to belong and deny what was happening.
I turned to Christianity in an attempt to find connection. I would spend hours sitting in quiet churches, drinking in the mystery, the solitude. I thought of becoming a nun when I was old enough.
One evening, while the twilight grew into darkness, I heard a banging noise as I was walking down the street toward my favorite cathedral. I approached the stone steps slowly to find a very worn and dirty man pounding on the large oak doors that led into the church.

16

"Please, please let me in. I'm so cold."

I could see that his coat was worn and threadbare, too light for this chilly winter evening.

"Please," he begged. "Have you anything to eat?"

Suddenly, my body shuddered with an overwhelming sense of anguish. I knew I could imagine how he was feeling, but this was more than imagination. I could feel his hunger, his aching body. These impressions were so intense that I was momentarily stunned.

The door opened a crack and the robed figure of a clergyman looked out. I could see the candles throwing a golden glow over the satiny surface of the pews, the altar shining in its brilliance, the church surrounded by the dark city night.

"Go away, we're closed," came the harsh response to the man's pleas. I froze.

"Go away and stop banging on the door!" And the door was slammed shut.

The beggar slowly turned and trudged off.

His pain and hopelessness flooded over me and I felt the slamming door like a clap of thunder from the heavens. In that moment, my psyche opened and I was filled with another person's experience as if it was my own. This was too much for me.

Suffering, irritation and anger swirled through my mind in a confused and chaotic dance. It wasn't clear who was feeling which emotion. This was the 1960s and if this was what "being open to the universe" meant, I wanted no part of it.

I stood on that cold downtown street trying to find my own feelings and, rather than embracing and welcoming this experience of psychic opening, I closed my mind and tried to forget that it was even possible.

MIND OVER MATTER

"Why do I have to have goose grease? I want Vick's VapoRub like everyone else!" I whined.

To no avail, however. My chest was plastered with a thick coating of fat. Sometimes it would be a mustard poultice, at

17

other times onions. It was almost enough to prevent me from being sick, just to avoid the treatment.

The story of my childhood could be encapsulated in these three words: mind over matter. My mother still practised the old healing arts, and the Christmas goose was always rendered to goose grease for our chests when we had a cold.

Mom's voice echoes down the years to me even now. "It's just mind over matter," she would say, any time I was ill and "Look at your reflection in the mirror and tell yourself you are not sick any more. The body listens to what your mind tells it."

Often, when my brother and I came home from school complaining about some teacher or acquaintance in very negative words and tone, she would say "Keep that up and you'll make yourself sick." It took me years to really understand what she meant about the connection between "what we think" and "what we are," or how our biography becomes our biology as Carolyn Myss says in her book *The Creation of Health*. Negative attitudes about life diminish the life force itself. And thus our resistance to disease is diminished.

I never quite believed in this power of mind over matter until I was in Grade Twelve. On a winter morning in late November, I was bundled up on the living room hide-a-bed, too sick to go to school, too sick to even walk up the stairs to my room.

"How are you feeling?" came the repeated question from my parents, every few hours, either by phone from work or standing beside my sickbed. I had come down with severe tonsillitis and mononucleosis, the kissing disease. Even in my illness, I thought that was funny since I didn't have a boyfriend.

My parents were anxiously awaiting my recovery so we could fly off to Hawaii for our Christmas vacation. We were supposed to leave in early December, but that was looking very unlikely unless a miracle happened. I was so weak I couldn't hold a spoon to feed myself. My doctor had suggested taking me there to recover, but I had to be well enough to fly.

The day before we were to leave the illness worsened. "Oh, no," wailed my mother, "your temperature's gone up to 104. What are we going to do?"

The bed that had been my home for the last few weeks was bathed in winter sunlight, weak and pale compared to the sunshine of Hawaii.

"I think what we'll do is this," said my dad, who always needed a plan. "If she has made significant improvement overnight, you fly to Hawaii tomorrow on the 10:00 AM flight; we'll follow in two weeks once she's recovered."

Ever hopeful, my parents were trying to plan a miracle. The thermometer appeared again with the next day's dawn.

"Oh, no, it's still 104. I'm not going," Mom announced. Then 15 minutes later she took my temperature again. Still 104°F.

More than anything in my 18 years of life I wanted Mom to catch that plane and have her extra two weeks bathed by sea and sun. She longed for this annual holiday all year, playing Hawaiian music every Saturday to accompany our weekly house cleaning. She had a strong call to Hawaii and had wanted to study tropical medicine when she was growing up, before poverty cut her dream short.

Every 15 minutes that thermometer took the score. "Still 104." she would say. Finally she decided that 9:00 AM was zero hour. If my temperature wasn't down by then she would stay home. The tension and anticipation were high, to say the least.

I focussed, I prayed, I talked to my body, I talked to the fairies, I talked to everybody and everything I could think of, even my bed, to help lower my temperature. Fifteen minutes before zero hour came the jubilant shriek.

"It's 98.6 on the nose!"

My father came running into the room to retake it, just in case Mom had made a mistake.

In fact, it was 98.6°F. Completely normal.

Mom finished the last-minute packing, loaded her bags into the car and my dad took her to catch her flight. The house settled into welcome calmness after the tension of the morning. I lay in bed reflecting on what had happened and giving thanks to any and all for this amazing turn of events.

When my dad returned from the airport he took my temperature again. It was 104°F. I had managed to bring it down but couldn't hold it there. My strong determination had empowered mind over matter and enabled Mom to wing towards her greatest love, Hawaii.

"Well, we'll have to phrase the telegrams very carefully so we don't worry her, and we don't lie" said my dad. The next two weeks were spent crafting telegrams to my mother. I was still too weak to walk unaided onto the plane, so my dad carried me, wrapped in a blanket, to my seat.

Maybe it was luck, maybe a broken thermometer. Or, maybe it was the intense focus and strong intention of a very determined girl that shifted the energy of my body for just long enough to accomplish what I wanted with all my heart, for Mom to have that time in Hawaii.

The next year the doctor suggested my tonsils be removed. Everything went well with the operation but my throat began to hemorrhage the next morning. Bleeding for hours before the staff took me up to the operating room, I remember a sense of unreality as I watched the overhead light fixtures flash by. Dimly I heard a nurse say, "Do you think she's going to make it," and then I was floating above the operating table, watching as they worked to stop the excessive bleeding.

There was an odd feeling of lightness yet I still had a sense of myself. I was curious about the body I could see lying there. This lasted only a moment, the blink of an eye.

Then, with an abrupt "twang," I was back in my body and coughing blood over the nurses and operating implements. The detachment was the most intriguing aspect — no pain, no fear, no worry, just a calm serenity and grace.

CHAPTER THREE

FARTHER AFIELD

NORTHERN SUMMERS

FROM THE TROPICAL beaches of Hawaiian winters, my life led me to a year-long adventure in Europe, exploring the landscapes, sacred sites like Stonehenge and Glastonbury and the intricately woven tapestry of my family history.

That year was a retrospective, a series of encounters with people and places that revealed the pictures of my ancestors and the land they had traveled. From the Greek Temple of Poseidon on the shores of the Mediterranean, feeling the antics of the gods rising with the morning sun, to the castle that was once in my family on the cliffs at Gower Bay in Wales, to the windmills of Holland, turning with stories from the war years of my dad and the liberation of Holland, the pattern and energy of my family came to life. As I traveled and heard the stories about my ancestors, my experience was enriched with subtle impressions, faint sounds, and distant feelings. If I was really quiet, the sounds of those times became superimposed over present-day sounds.

With my return to Vancouver, a new chapter began, one that would lead me into the far northern regions of Arctic North America to discover a land beyond magic, a land that expresses the primordial energy of our past. This silent land would teach me, would define me, would show me about myself, and about the magic and mystery of life.

This adventure began as I married and settled down to support my new husband in his university studies in anthropology and archaeology. Psychic experiences were the furthest things from my mind in those full days of work and play, when Duncan and I were starting to dream and build our future together.

One evening after dinner in Vancouver, we were sitting in the spring air, watching the petals fall from a Japanese cherry tree outside our apartment window, showering the ground like confetti at Earth's wedding, when Duncan remarked, "You know, one of my anthropology professors is looking for crew on an expedition he's leading to the North Slope of Alaska. He wants to do some archaeological excavations looking for evidence of early man. It's going to be the summer before we move to Calgary. We'd leave in May and return at the end of August. What do you think? Should we go?"

As if there was any other choice, I thought. Who could turn that adventure down?

And then the anticipated reality hit! What was I agreeing to? Spending three months isolated in the wilderness — tenting, no fresh food, no phone, none of the things I took for granted growing up in the city with parents who were, very definitely, city dwellers.

We had decided that once Duncan received his university degree, we would move to Calgary where he could continue in graduate studies in archaeology and I could resume my studies in ecology and anthropology. This field trip seemed like an amazing opportunity.

So there we were, driving our little orange Volkswagen Beetle along the dusty gravel of the Alcan Highway into the May mornings. We traveled in a caravan, just like the gypsies, a crew of seven plus the director, Leon; his ten-year-old son; his co-director, Vicki, a free-spirited graduate student from Boston; and my cat Blue, camping each night as the meandering highway led us towards our destination, Fairbanks, Alaska, and our summer's work of uncovering the footprints of the past.

Fairbanks, in the early 1970s, was still a frontier town, not yet booming from the influx of petroleum workers and oil company money. Our task was to survey a portion of the Saganirvirktok Valley, on the route of the pipeline, for prehistoric sites, with the hope of finding evidence of Early Man in the New World, the first peoples across the Bering Strait land bridge, the gateway between Siberia and Alaska.

We bought food for three months and packed it in 14-day amounts based on a fixed menu that would repeat every two weeks. With this plan, the plane could re-supply our camp every two weeks. We had no on-going support in Fairbanks and no radio or way of communicating with the outside world, so our well-being depended on planning and organization.

Taking off into the clouds on a drenching afternoon in late May, our pilot flew the small prop plane north across the remote forests to the tundra, and the stark rock of the Brooks Range close to the top of the world. Still covered with patches of winter snow, the rocky grey stretches of this Arctic mountain landscape pointed sharp ridges and spines toward the heavens.

"No trees," I kept saying to Duncan. "There are no trees here." I had known that there wouldn't be any trees, but hadn't realized what that really meant in terms of the land. There was a stark, angular beauty to mountain and valley; no edges softened by soil and grass, no roundness, nothing hidden by forest. I was stunned by the rawness of the landscape, by its presence. No touch of civilization diminished it. With no words to describe what I was experiencing, I busied myself with Blue rather than engage in the excited chatter of my fellow passengers.

Leon had chosen to locate our camp on an esker beside a fresh-water lake. This was a perfect camping site, a dry gravel ridge some ten to twelve feet above the boggy tundra. Here, the flat Arctic plain of the North Slope was beginning to build into

23

the alpine reaches of the mountain range. On that esker, I realized I was standing on stones that lay exactly as the last glacier had left them, many centuries ago.

I had studied glaciers in school; now I would live on a remnant of glacial activity. It was no surprise to find that other valley dwellers had camped in that spot long before us. Fire-cracked rock and projectile points scattered the gravel surface. In some aspects, humans are very predictable.

We laid out the camp with the cook tent at the center and our sleeping tents scattered along the esker like small, glacial boulders, close enough for comfort yet still maintaining some privacy. After a hearty dinner, we sat around the Coleman lantern sharing our hopes and fears for this summer. It would be 12 weeks before we saw another person, outside of our pilot. Or, so we thought that evening.

The site to excavate was high in a saddle on the side of the surrounding foothills, the perfect spot for a lookout. Leon was hoping to find clear evidence of pre-Clovis Man in the New World — the first people to occupy this continent. The barren, empty tundra stretched for hundreds of miles in every direction, our tent camp an outlier of humankind in this vast expanse of sedge, willow and caribou.

Nothing had prepared me for this stark beauty and majesty. The Arctic regions of North America are wondrous lands, empty of the major trappings of civilization, inhabited by a small population of hardy individuals. We were privileged to witness the valley in its last days of life as a wilderness.

As camp cook for the initial part of the summer, I was the first one up in the morning. I would push the sleeping body of my cat out of the sleeping bag and reach underneath to retrieve the clothes that had been kept warm there. I dressed in many layers before venturing out into the Alaskan sunrise, the sun like milky water in the morning mist. Slowly undoing the zipper on my tent, I would savor the calm stillness of the morning quiet. My body was slowing down finally from the jangled rush of city noise.

Crossing the threshold of my tent was like moving into the surreal world of visionary painters, a world devoid of all sound

The archaeological crew in Alaska. The site of the excavation was up in the saddle at the left end of the hill.

or scent of civilization. The mist would be rising from the tundra, casting a haze over the golden rays of the rising sun. As the modern world slipped farther and farther away from me, the mystical nature of the land emerged.

BECOMING QUIET

Spending all day in camp, I used cooking as a diversion and distraction from the incessant noise and chatter in my mind. Sometimes fear would arise and I would become lost in the loneliness, the apparent reality of this isolation. Even though I had been raised a Buddhist, my meditation skills were not up to this challenge. There were times when I thought my mental dialogue would drive me insane. I went for long walks, I talked to Blue, I talked to God, I shrieked at the mosquitoes.

The Alaskan tundra taught of the vast expanse of landscape that was our world before cityscapes sprouted throughout the

25

wilderness. We were a tiny tenting microcosm in the immense, self-sustaining Arctic world — interlopers, intruders. We tried to maintain our southern nine-to-five work ethic in the face of 24-hour daylight and deteriorating weather by summer's end. We would get up at 7:30 AM, have breakfast at 8:00, then get off to the site by 8:45. A full day's work with two coffee breaks and an hour for lunch would find us back at camp for supper at 6:00 PM. Field notes and chores would occupy us until bedtime around 10:00; all in the broad daylight of the Arctic summer. While our physiological rhythms were adapting to the rhythm of the land, we superimposed an artificial schedule and maintained our separation from the natural world.

As I spent more and more time alone, I began to notice my surroundings. When I could quiet my mind, I got a sense that the land was full of energy and life, and I was beginning to feel in my body the currents and shifting tides of this environment. As my mind became quiet, my body responded with deeper resonance to the energies of this wild landscape, no longer needing to reflect the cacophony of the city. In some ways I realized that the city was a very tame environment; loud, raucous, and hectic but tame nonetheless. The wilderness flowed with an intensity that felt as though it came from the fiery core of the Earth itself.

We started to feel what the wind was going to do before it happened; cloud movements became the dialogues between Earth and sky and we watched them intently for rain. Even though I had checked the weather each morning before leaving for work in Vancouver, this was different. We almost became one with the weather, with the land, with the shifting and changing. Our small city lives had expanded to include the immediacy of the natural world around us.

I was learning about a quiet mind — getting rid of the chatter in order to hear the messages, an invitation into "becoming" the land, into sensing energy psychically. It was a much deeper opening than any I had had previously. I was beginning to experience things around me with the sixth sense of knowing.

Dyan, the camp cook.

WOLF

There she was again, out on the tundra watching our camp. Every morning for the last week she had been standing there, watching. As I made my way to the outhouse in the early morning after rising from my warm and cozy sleeping bag, I looked for her. She would stand there, so still, for a few minutes, then lope off to disappear into the horizon. Maybe it was the outhouse that caught her interest, at first.

Located on the edge of the esker so that it was shielded on three sides from camp and open towards the north, the outhouse provided a view up the valley and out onto the North Slope itself. It stood as silent evidence to man's need for privacy and convention in the boundless reaches of treeless tundra. The tallest object in sight, it was made from two-by-four lengths of wood draped with orange plastic tarps, and sported a white plastic toilet seat suspended on a metal frame over a large hole in the ground. The morning was quiet there, before anyone else had crawled out of their sleeping bags in search of breakfast.

As far as my eye could see the view was full of grassy green hummocks and icy streamlets under the blue morning sky. Cold as it was, the beauty filled me with radiant warmth. One morning while I was sitting there, contemplating the beauty of what lay before me, the river to the left flowing at the foot of a series of velvety green hills and the high saddle of our site on the mountain ridge to the right, I saw her.

There, straight ahead, an Arctic wolf. That first morning my stomach jumped up to my throat. I did my best to swallow it back to where it belonged and took a very deep breath.

"Hello wolf," was all I could manage to croak, and then chatted on in my nervousness about who we were and what we were doing here. I was completely unable to move, so talking seemed to be the next best thing.

She stood for what seemed like an hour and then loped away. To maintain my stillness was quite a challenge, sitting on that outhouse seat with my jeans and long underwear down around my ankles. Just how could I run away from this experience, even if I had wanted to?!

I began to watch for her. She came, every morning, always a little closer. I would talk about what we were doing and inquire about her and her life in this vast land. She continued to come closer each day until we were only ten or twelve feet apart. She was beautiful, curious and wild.

I wasn't sure what was happening in those morning moments. I told the rest of the crew in the beginning, but after their first glance, warm sleeping bags were more important than an Arctic wolf.

She had stillness about her, a stillness of energy that reflected the silence of the land and, even with my chatter, I was conscious of trying to tune in, to resonate with her. I kept wondering, "What does this wolf have to teach me? Why has she come?"

Eventually, I saw that as I kept chattering each day, she just stood there, still and mindful. Her beauty, her presence were vibrant reflections of the wilderness itself. As I rambled on each morning, her ears would twitch, and she'd tilt her head to catch the sound. Comfort grew between us.

Psychic resonance was certainly part of this encounter. Here I was, isolated, with wilderness as my constant companion, and now this wolf had come. I reached out to her with my consciousness. There was so little interference from other sources — radios, people, telephones — all the psychic noise of a populated area. It was quiet enough that even with my lack of experience I could "find" her psychically.

I wanted to know her and I was so curious that no thought of harm to either her or myself had entered my mind, only of opening the doorway where we might meet each other at the threshold between two worlds.

As she approached one morning I could sense her nervousness. She came closer and closer, and I could see that she was carrying something in her mouth. She approached me cautiously, nervously, until she could drop her gift three feet away from me, a prize of immense value in this fragile land, a freshly killed ground squirrel.

My world stopped. I was captivated. In that instant our eyes met, held, and we spoke. My body experienced that conversation, one that my mind could not even imagine, let alone comprehend.

Two days later she brought her pups with her. The four little bundles of cream-colored energy were playful as they bounded around her legs. She waited while I got prepared, and then led her pups, with me following, back to her den. Breakfast for the crew would be late that morning.

Not knowing what else to do, I followed my intuition. There were no other guidelines. I watched the pups play around the den's entrance, delighted at the opportunity to glimpse, and to sense, the world of this wild creature.

She came alone the next morning and stood solemnly for a long time, watching. I knew to say goodbye. I saw her in the distance from time to time over the rest of the summer and always sent her thoughts of respect and honor.

I found that in those interactions with the wolf, the everyday world was far distant, leaving only the present and the guidance flowing through the stillness. In those moments my mind was quiet and I was one with all around me. My psychic sensing was sharpened; it was beginning to develop into awareness that went deeply into the energy of everything around me.

Contrasts were everywhere: the turmoil and angst within the crew set against the exquisite harmony of the Arctic ecosystem; the frantic distractions and busyness against the smooth flow of life on the tundra; and the pettiness of our egos, our personalities, set against the grandeur and majesty of the spirit of the land. In every direction space yielded to the infinite.

Time in the Arctic moves to a different clock, a clock run by seasons, by weather and by the moods of the land itself. Living all my life in the big city, I was so separate from this natural world, I had no idea of its mystery or of the energies that flowed through it and enlivened it.

THE ROCKY RAFT

We moved camp in the middle of the season to another site about 20 miles farther into the mountains. The fresh-water lake outside the door of the cook tent reflected the snow-topped granite peaks that surrounded us and the grassy Arctic tundra grew again on its crystal clear surface. Leon and Vicki had chosen this campsite because of the lake and its serenity. The only disadvantage was that the site for excavating was about a mile and a half away across a fast-flowing, 20-foot-wide river. We had no raft or boat to use in the crossing. Improvisation was needed in many ways that summer and so we set about designing a raft made of empty five-gallon metal fuel cans and the thickest willow branches we could find. Arctic willow on the tundra grows as a bush about four feet high and even though decades old, the branches seldom reach more than wrist size. Our engineering feat was successful and we would pull each other across the river on this raft. Miraculously, it lasted to the end of the field season although the cans slowly took on water and the raft sank infinitesimally each day.

Stepping onto the raft was always an expression of trust: trust in God perhaps, trust in the thin string that we used to pull the raft across the river, certainly. Each day we would complete that journey twice, depending on the chord that held us safely between the shores. Each time I couldn't help but think of the tenuous connections that we hold during our journey across the river of life.

Blue had watched us all summer, as we headed out each morning toward the site. She was usually content to stay in the cook tent with whomever was on duty that day or curled up deep in a down sleeping bag in one of the tents. We had decided to rotate cooking to give everyone an opportunity to spend a quiet day alone in camp. On this particular day, Blue was determined

The raft on which the crew crossed the river every day.

to leave camp with us. As Billy tried to hold her, she scratched his hand in a strenuous attempt to get free. She walked, tail held high as only a Siamese cat can, all the way with us. And then she saw the river, and the raft. Her body froze at the sight, her tail puffed out and the hair stood up along her back.

A frozen, startled cat, she looked like a cartoon character with her hair exploding, in the middle of the Arctic tundra, about to embark on a journey few cats would consider as reasonable in any of their lifetimes. Determination strong, she very tentatively stepped onto the raft, when our turn came. I talked to her all the way across and steadied her when the raft was rocky, both with my voice and with my energy. It was strange that she wouldn't let me hold her. This was something she was going to do herself.

The cat, Blue, the day she went with the crew to the excavation site. The Brooks Range is in the background.

She walked proudly up the bank on the other side, sniffed around the area, and then curled up and slept until it was time to leave, some six hours later. She didn't object to being carried for the return raft ride. She rode inside my parka, her head just peeking out under my chin. Her interest had been satisfied and she never left camp again until the plane flight to civilization.

Between Blue and the wolf, I wondered about consciousness that summer, living so close to the natural world. What is it, where is it? I realized it wasn't just the domain of humanity but I didn't have any answers, just observations.

Consciousness was very evident in Blue's behavior. This was not instinct, no Pavlovian stimulus-response behavior. Her focus, commitment and desire to come with us that day, in a very "four-year-old" manner, were obvious and seemingly based on clear choice and a conscious awareness of the rhythm and pattern of life. Blue and the wolf had painted a picture for me of a world not so foreign from our own. Yet I hesitated to ascribe human interpretation to animal behavior, still caught in the duality and separation of our view of this world where humans are above all else on Earth.

SEEING THE UNSEEN

At the first campsite, some of us had begun to have strange dreams of other times and places. One night I dreamed of four men, rough and dark, dressed in skins. Seated around a smoldering fire, they formed a council of elders who had lived in this valley. One sat farther away in the background. Vicki said that was a sign in the psychic world of distance in relation to time. They said that they were the original inhabitants. Showing an archaeological site that was empty of artifacts, they said we would not find what we were looking for, as they didn't like our director and his intentions for the use of the material. That night, Leon woke up and grabbed his gun, feeling a menacing energy in his tent.

We turned to Vicki for her interpretations. "It's information from the spirit world," she would say. "We've been asking why we haven't found any artifacts yet, and now they have answered."

The more work we did on the first site we were to excavate that summer, the clearer it became that it was sterile. We had found no artifacts at all, other than a few pieces of fire-cracked rock. The site on which we were camped, which was not being excavated, held more artifacts, and more information, than the one that we had worked on hopefully for the first half of the summer. We were looking in the wrong place.

Vicki talked about intention in those days under the Alaskan clouds. "Be clear and pay attention," she would admonish us. The idea of being in charge of our reality was new to me. I had always felt at the mercy of the spirit world when I received the many impressions from around me. Thinking that I was a victim to this psychic sight, I tried through my reluctance to shut it off. Yet what we resist, persists.

We were learning about the clarity and purpose of our intention, our personal agendas. Vicki taught us that when we operate solely for our own gain, the spirit world is unlikely to fully support us in achieving our goals. Leon got the funding and the tactical support, and organized the crew to launch this major program but this site was sterile and in that the project was a failure.

We moved camp to a new location in the middle of the summer so that we were closer to the second site, stretched along the river bank. We had started excavating five two-by-two-metre pits using trowels and dustpans to remove the thin Arctic soil in ten-centimetre layers. Each stone flake, each projectile point, each bone chip that was found was measured in place. This site was full of artifacts, each unlike the previous one. It was a painstakingly slow procedure, sifting through the layers of the past, yet one filled with the excitement of unexpected discoveries.

Later in the summer, Vicki, Simon and I devised a game to take our minds off the approaching cold and snow of fall and winter. After each ten-centimetre level was completed, the three of us would gather around the edge of the pit and try to guess what artifacts lay below in the next ten centimetres. We would stand there, intent, with eyes focussed on the smooth surface. After gazing for a few moments, we would sketch the layout of artifacts as we "saw" them below the soil. After the level was excavated we would compare our drawings with the actual distribution of artifacts that were found.

It was practice at seeing in a psychic way for all of us and was fun, thanks to Vicki. She was exploring all of the psychic areas in her life, and we often gathered around her as she laid out her tarot cards in the midnight sun.

She would do readings and we would watch and ask questions and she began to teach us the tarot. And the more I watched, the more I could see that this was a way into our consciousness, into those answers that we longed for and are unable to discern.

I began to do readings to explore the cards and the messages they held. Doing readings for Vicki, I always saw fire. I thought it was her fiery nature, her incredible presence, her free spirit, until two years later when I found out that she and her new baby had died in a hotel fire, burned to death before they could escape. I decided then, when I got that news, that I didn't want to expand this sight any more than I already had.

Did I really want to know, when you can see what is going to happen and are seemingly unable to change it? Knowledge can be a great gift, information for decisions and yet, I wondered then if our lives aren't in some way pre-programmed when we're born. That we're here to learn whatever it is we've come here to learn, and we'll learn it one way or another, whether it's through hotel fires, the fire of relationship, the fire of struggle or the fire of joy.

In some ways we experience the process of death and rebirth every night when we fall asleep and wake to a new day. That Arctic summer I thought a lot about these things in the quiet, when everybody else was at the site and I was in the tent making bread, in the stillness, in the quiet, listening to the birds, the mosquitoes — always the mosquitoes.

I could feel a tangible insignificance while walking out of sight of camp through the immense energy and beauty of this particular complex ecosystem. I tried to walk softly, knowing that any disturbance of the fragile setting would take hundreds of years to recover. Time moved slowly, more in harmony with the cycles of the Earth, the spirals of the climate, more in tune with the still-ness of eternity.

And silence, the privilege of silence — to walk for hours across the tundra, cradled in the deep well of the sky, without distrac-tion. To come to know the rhythms of life; the myriad facets of the climate etched across the face of the land; the dwellers of the Earth and sky, their integral part in the complete landscape; and to begin to catch a glimpse of the true nature of environment, one that spoke strongly of the Spirit of Place, the palpable energy held within the shape of a landscape.

I came to know the land and all that was in it as a living, complex being and in that awareness, my vision and apprecia-tion of this planet changed forever. This land had entered my soul and Nature became my solace, my refuge, my heartbeat.

We moved to Calgary after that summer to continue our graduate work at the university. Studying in the Faculty of Science, where everything was concerned with analysis and scientific proof, I longed for similar analytical proof of the psychic realm I was experiencing. The duality of these worlds,

Archaeological camp on Banks Island.

Musk-oxen on Banks Island, with the Masik River in the background.

the scientific and the psychic, created some confusion in my life, especially when I was overcome by another person's intense emotion.

During these years, we traveled on other archaeological expeditions to Banks Island in the Canadian Arctic, surveying archaeologically unknown areas, far from any northern settlements.

I found that I could scan an area psychically while we were surveying and simply walk over to evidence of a site — a projectile point or fire-cracked rock, for example. I had no idea how this happened or what I did to receive the information. It was like looking at a map, a map of a landscape just beyond the physical, and being able to sense what was on the ground.

Those summers deepened my appreciation for the land and its mystery while providing me with a brief respite of quiet solitude in the busy time of university and work. I loved to hike alone to our fishing lake about two miles from camp. The Arctic char were so curious they would follow the lure in to shore before striking. We supplemented our freeze-dried food with fresh char and salads made from sorrel and other natural greens.

Walking across the tundra to the fishing lake in the bright sunshine after a day of excavating made the mosquitoes and cold worthwhile. Nowhere else could I walk unafraid, no other person for hundreds of miles, just the caribou and musk-ox and the occasional Arctic fox darting behind a willow bush. The tundra was alive with birds that summer; whistling swans and sandhill cranes were the most spectacular. The cry of the loons haunted our days and nights.

These long months in the high Arctic also brought challenges as we pushed the boundaries of our physical endurance. Some of these were anticipated, like the mosquitoes and the wind, others were welcome gifts, while still others were completely unexpected.

TUKTU

Tuktu was the ice-blue-eyed malamute that I had brought down to Calgary from Banks Island where she had been raised. Part wolf, she was a constant reminder of the Arctic and the events that happened during the last summer I spent there. She had been with us for the field season and her owners had given her to me.

We were on the south coast of Banks Island, hiking back to Sachs Harbour in the chill air of late August. We had been on an archaeological expedition at the Masik River site for the last four months and now it was time to go home, back to university, back to Calgary.

Archaeologically, the summer had been exceptional. The site had been productive and intriguing in its uniqueness. Arrowheads like the ones we found there had not been described in the literature before. This site was a first.

Psychologically, the summers were tough. The cold, the isolation and the mosquitoes got to us after a few weeks. This particular summer, two young men of our crew had had personal trouble. Neither was experienced with isolation and they had

At an excavation site on Banks Island: Dyan second from left. (COURTESY OF DR. CHARLES ARNOLD)

been surprised by how strongly they reacted, both thinking they would freeze to death in the isolated wilderness.

Their months of fear of an icy death almost became a reality as we hiked back to Sachs Harbour. Two anthropologists had come out in their boat to offer us a ride back to the town, a day's boat ride away. Rob and Dave had gladly accepted their offer: anything to get out of the last days of hiking. They packed their gear in the boat, and climbed in with broad smiles and friendly waves, knowing a hot meal awaited them when they arrived in town.

We watched as the small powerboat headed out into the gulf. Clouds were down on the water at the horizon, and we knew there was ice out there. Amundsen Gulf at this time of year held small ice floes still left from last year's pack ice. We wished them luck with our goodbye waves, and turned back to resume our hike.

About an hour after they left, I noticed Tuktu. Standing on the edge of the cliff, she was gazing out to sea, looking at something beyond my sight. I could sense her anxiety and growing restlessness. Something had happened out there, at sea, something that she could sense, before we even noticed anything amiss. She would come over to us, whine, and then race back to the water's edge. Her concern was overwhelming to me and I felt her anxiety in my own body. With no radio, we could only wonder what was happening, and we wondered for the next five hours.

Then we saw the small plane, slowly tracing a search pattern along the coastline. Something must have happened to the small boat that was carrying our crew and the anthropologists through the icy water.

We spent the night tossing and turning, worrying. About three o'clock in the morning Tuktu stopped her pacing, settled down and went to sleep. I, on the other hand, continued to worry.

Late the next afternoon, a freighter canoe came out from Sachs Harbour to pick us up and brought the news that our crew members were safe. Their boat had hit an ice floe and sunk. An unlikely circumstance had put a small plane at the airport for refueling, so the search began immediately after someone

Tuktu. (COURTESY OF DR. CHARLES ARNOLD)

noticed they had not arrived by the time they were supposed to. Plucked from the ice floe, they were close to hypothermia and frostbite, but in time, they recovered completely.

Tuktu knew, through some sense more highly tuned than ours, or less blocked perhaps. She knew the moment they got into trouble, and relaxed as soon as they were rescued — at three o'clock in the weak light of the Arctic dawn.

I didn't think much of my previous encounters with the "unseen" realms. They could be explained away by imagination, stories I had heard somewhere, make-believe. Watching Tuktu I could see that there was something going on here, some kind of awareness that was beyond my usual senses, an energy outside normal perception. I couldn't explain this away through make-believe.

Animals are much more in tune and at ease with this sixth sense than we are, although we can awaken it with practice. Perhaps we have to open to some ancient part of ourselves, a part more in tune with nature and the energies around us.

I wanted to know more. I wanted to explore this. I wanted to experience this level of awareness. And with that wanting, my life changed — again.

WATCH WHAT YOU ASK FOR!

Duncan had finished his graduate work and it was time to move on. We went skiing in the Rocky Mountains the day before his thesis defence in an attempt to relieve the stress and pressure of the impending examination.

As we sat on a ledge high up a logging road eating lunch, I began to dream of our future and the new life it held. Looking out to the snow-covered horizon, I was sure we would be moving soon, after I finished my graduate work. I could see moving to a large city far from Calgary and as I let my mind drift in wondering, I could also see the start of a family, a small baby. I was surprised by that idea; children had seldom come up in discussions of our future together. I smiled at the idea, then let the thought pass as we resumed our skiing trip.

41

Duncan passed his defence the next day and was offered a job at the University of Toronto, a much larger city than Calgary. We decided to accept even though it was only a two-year contract. I awoke a few mornings later to a voice in my head that said, "Hi, Mommy, I'm here." Just days after that, I discovered that I was pregnant. The child that I had seen became a reality. I enjoyed talking to this small spirit each morning as I awoke. Sometimes I could hear him reply but I always put it down to imagination.

We moved to Toronto in time for the start of the school year and I returned to Calgary to finish my Master's thesis. When it was complete in October I moved back to Toronto to begin life there. Fixing up our home was fun, the first house we had owned, and with our baby due in March it became a great adventure.

Many of the experiences of my pregnancy, and this time in general, were related to the body-mind connection. It was clear during my labor that my intellect had no experience in directing the process of birth and that my body was the product of millennia of successful births. Therefore, my scientific nature said, "Listen to your body, not your mind." What was paramount was to move into the stillness, to silence the frantic chatter of my mind and let my body respond with its innate and awesome wisdom.

After our son Devin was born, I could still not see the opportunity to develop my psychic skills. I often knew when he was waking or falling asleep even if I was far away. I would use the phone to check and verify what I was sensing. I put this down to the mother-baby connection, however. Having shared an envelope of energy for nine months and developed in concert with each other, most mothers and babies are psychically connected.

There is a maxim that "energy follows attention." My intuition was trying to get my attention but I was denying this psychic unfolding and focussing solely on the physical and material world. I was definitely out of balance.

One terrible day I was driving on the freeway with nine-month-old Devin when my vision began to fade. A hole appeared in the center of the picture that I usually see, the visual field, and slowly, inexplicably, grew larger, leaving only transparent redness. I watched my world begin to dissolve right before my very eyes figuratively and literally. I rubbed my eyes, scratched my eyelids, and frantically rolled my eyes from side to side, attempting to dislodge the growing red veil.

Still driving, I was praying for an exit ramp before my world was completely gone. The intense feeling of panic gave way to shock as my vision continued to deteriorate, all within a matter of moments. The sage who said, "Our world can change in the blink of an eye" was truly prophetic for me that day.

All I could think of was Devin strapped into his carseat behind me. I prayed with every fiber of my being to get home safely with my tiny baby. I prayed over and over, every prayer I had ever heard. They were answered and I breathed a sigh of relief when I stopped the car in front of our home and carried Devin into the house.

Within an hour I could not see through my right eye. It was like looking through a piece of red cellophane, except there was nothing beyond. I was thankful that my left eye was untouched, then.

I phoned my doctor to make an appointment for the next day. He sent me to a specialist who could offer no explanation — nor any hope. I was completely devastated; worried about how I would look after my young son, and how I would contribute to our family, especially financially. I was left without direction, no straws to grasp.

With the passage of several weeks, the vision in my right eye improved, but an intense pain developed in my left eye and within days I had lost all vision in that eye. Here I was in a new city with a baby and only partial sight. I was terrified.

The only place I could turn for help was my spirituality and I prayed that my vision would be restored so that I could function. I was so afraid that I trembled with panic and the fear was so great it blocked any opportunity to explore my other senses.

I was afraid, the way we often are when facing a serious illness. I just wanted to get better, to pretend this was not happening. I didn't know enough in the late 1970s to ask the questions about what messages were held in this illness. I desperately wanted to put it behind me and get on with life.

My right eye continued to improve until I was able to look after my family, drive and do the normal things of life. Each morning I would open my eyes after a prayer asking for sight, yet I wouldn't "see" the sight that was being offered.

Most disease holds a gift that brings us greater understanding about our way of being and what might be out of balance in our life. The experience of blindness offered many choices and indications about how I wanted to live in the world. My choice seemed to concern the depth that I willing to "see" and whether or not I was willing to acknowledge this psychic sight completely.

In retrospect I could see that I had been choosing to live with no depth perception, seeing the world as a flat surface, seeing from one perspective only, having a blind side, being blind-sided as they say in business. I seemed to prefer to struggle along blindly, ignoring the psychic sight which could have brought an added dimension of grace and ease to my life.

Two years after this experience of blindness I felt a shower of sparks cascade throughout my abdomen. "Now what?" I wondered. I paused for a moment and thought back over the last few days. "Could I be pregnant again?" Sure enough, the cascading lights signaled the arrival of our second son, Aiden. With eyes that sparkled, he was always into everything, fearless and provocative in exploring his world, the source of much laughter and many grey hairs.

Even though we had settled into a comfortable family life in Toronto, Duncan and I knew that his contracts at the university would soon end. We talked about our various options and decided to move to the Northwest Territories after a job offer came from the territorial government.

CHAPTER FOUR

RECOGNIZING THE GIFT

TO THE EDGE

"AND THE TEMPERATURE is a balmy -55°C and falling," the voice crackled across the aircraft as our plane descended into Yellowknife in the sub-Arctic regions of Canada. I looked at my two children, my sweet, two-year-old son, Devin and my new baby, Aiden, only seven weeks old, softly asleep in their blankets, and realized that the heaviest of their Toronto clothes would never shut out that kind of cold. Leaving the warm, safe womb of the Lockheed Electra, we emerged into a surreal landscape of frozen fog hanging above icy dunes of windswept snow on the tarmac. My breath froze as soon as it left my lips and joined the already frozen world as I hurried toward the beckoning shelter of the tiny airport terminal building. I had come to the end of the Earth, the frigid icy blackness of the Arctic winter. It was the middle of January and I had just arrived at my new home.

The street lights cast a pale yellow glow through the ice fog that blanketed the town as I walked to the grocery store the next

45

morning. I was just about to cross the main street when I heard shouting in the distance. Out of the fog came a dogsled and musher, moving fast toward Great Slave Lake. The dogs' breath had crystallized into an icy ruff around their black noses and open, panting mouths as the musher called them to greater speed. Several more sleds followed, the dogs straining against their traces in an all-out effort to win the race. A colorful and unexpected introduction to the eccentricities and uniqueness of life in the north!

This land, where caribou outnumber people 20 to one and there are more lakes than caribou, epitomized precisely the sentiment of the Quebec song: "My country is not a country, it is the winter." The stark realities of the winter were in our thoughts, as we realized that new survival strategies would be needed here. On all levels — physical, mental, emotional and spiritual — this new land would require acceptance, self-responsibility and awareness. The Arctic exposes our vulnerability and challenges us to move beyond current ways of thought.

Being a homemaker with two small children, I enjoyed staying in touch with the archaeology of the north. It provided some mental stimulation. Because my Master's thesis had been on faunal analysis, the study of ancient bones from archaeological sites, I used to help Duncan with the material from his summer excavations in the Arctic.

With bone fragments spread across the dining room table, I was doing a first level sorting of material from a site on the Arctic coast. Dividing the bones into bird, sea mammal, caribou and "other" I noticed a peculiar quality of certain fragments. Some of the bones, particularly those in the "other" pile, felt different. When I picked up those fragments, they would almost burn my fingertips with a strange heat.

As I continued to work, I began to hear wailing and crying in the distance. I knew this wasn't from around my neighborhood and that my children were safe, having their afternoon naps. Definitely women's voices screaming, though. Knowing nothing about the site, I showed Duncan my work and asked him about the mysterious pile.

46

"I wondered if you would get a sense of that. They're human bones. The excavation suggests that the prehistoric people were massacred and cannibalized."

That explained the screaming and the intense vibration of the bone. The energy of the violence was somehow held within the bone itself.

A research study of the hunting patterns of people in small communities took me across the Northwest Territories, working closely with Native organizations, elders and hunters in the tiny Arctic settlements. Through this job I began to appreciate my father's lessons about tolerance and patience. I often remembered his words during frustrating, cross-cultural misunderstandings and seemingly endless confusion as two very different cultures tried to work together. I would often hear him whisper, "Gently, gently" in my ear when I was ready to explode in frustration.

Yet, I began to realize that here were a people who had lived in harmony with the rhythms of this land for thousands of years, with an unending connection to landscape. As Wade Davis notes in *Shadows in the Sun, Essays on the Spirit of Place*: "Just as landscape defines a people, culture springs from a spirit of place"[1] and I was certainly a displaced person. I was away from the landscape of southern Canada, which had defined me, and in a place which held an entirely new sense of spirit. Alaska came to mind often during the days that lay ahead.

While I thought I knew about the concept of right time — the "right" time to do things — I hadn't really experienced "right time" until I worked with the aboriginal people of the north. As a wildlife biologist in charge of the territory-wide research program, I had fieldworkers in each of the communities. Fort Rae was 100 kilometres from Yellowknife, and on one occasion I had arranged a meeting with my fieldworker and the tribal council for 9:00 AM. My technician, Ruth, and I borrowed a government car and drove out there early on a cold and icy Tuesday.

We arrived at the band office to find it empty except for a secretary. I asked her where everyone was, and she replied, "Hunting."

"Hunting?" I said. "We have a meeting at nine o'clock."

47

"Well, it was the right time to go hunting, so they chartered a plane and left for Contwoyto Lake early this morning. They'll be back tomorrow."

As Ruth and I drove back to Yellowknife, we were initially angry. Then we began to talk about this different concept of time and closeness to the land. We recalled how many times we had each felt that a particular day was right for something other than being in the office: perhaps it was the right day to work at home, or the right day to visit the Legislative Assembly. This was a small glimpse into another perception of reality, and the way that it structures their world.

The long nights of Yellowknife provided an opportunity for me to seek explanations for many of the unusual experiences in my life. I began to read books on paranormal activity and accounts by famous psychics like Edgar Cayce, but they didn't hold the quantifiable explanations that my scientific mind wanted. I wanted to know how they were happening but, even more, I wanted to know why — why me?

Caribou, the main food source for the hunting peoples of the Northwest Territories. (COURTESY OF DR. CHARLES ARNOLD)

ENERGY

Yellowknife was a time to think about healing the wounds of the past. As well as working as a wildlife biologist, I began volunteering as a group facilitator at the mental health clinic with a therapist named Gregg. I witnessed many miracles in the therapeutic and recovery groups. People were finally reconnecting with themselves and with their Higher Power, the source of their spiritual life: being in the right place at the right time to receive exactly what they were in need of, whether it was information or a hug; becoming open and vulnerable to others, and to themselves.

The women I worked with taught me by their very lives that one of the keys to our healing, to profound change and new ways of thinking, is to be accepting of the idea that we are in charge of creating our own reality. To be completely engaged in our lives and fully present to the relationships in which we are involved, to be undivided, unconcerned and trusting was the desired way. The trust of the Inuit women who had spent so much time on the land, living on migratory caribou as their main food source, was profound. They could never be certain that they could find caribou for food or that the weather would be clear enough to go hunting.

During one of the therapy groups, Gregg was leading a guided visualization that would enable the women to meet their spirit or power animals. I was monitoring the vibration of the group, paying attention to the energy field of each woman and watching their body language: slight facial movements and subtle hand gestures. I also got a sense of how the meditation was proceeding for each one. I then realized that I was following the meditation by imagining I was on a beach waiting for my spirit animal to appear.

It was a split image, a wavery picture, like the heat waves rising in the distance from the blacktop of a highway heated by the sun, superimposed on the more stable sight of the women sitting in a circle. I could see, looking down the beach, an animal approaching me. It was a honey-golden grizzly bear. She walked up to me, sniffed my face, then walked around behind me and lay

49

down. I was sitting on the beach, so I leaned against her. I could literally feel her fur against my back, and her breathing synchronize with mine — or mine with hers, I wasn't sure which. I could smell her scent around me. Bear walked with me for many years, and when I was in trouble or afraid, someone with bear energy would turn up to help: an incredibly powerful spirit, for which I was thankful on many occasions.

Through this meditation I began to actually, physically feel spirit energy around me. It seems that each body is a large tuning fork, which resonates with the energies around us, in this physical world and the more intangible metaphysical world.

Later the next year, an invitation came to join a Native healing circle. I already knew and had worked with several of the women involved in the circle, and I was honored to be asked. A healing circle is a spiritual gathering in which each person speaks from the heart and other members of the circle witness the experience rather than offering advice or trying to fix the problem being spoken about. People are free to share tears, joy, anger, and sadness as they feel ready, all in the safety of the circle.

I felt nervous as I walked up to the door of the house to attend my first circle. My friend Victoria, April, a Cree woman from the plains, and Laurie, a Louchou woman from Arctic Canada were powerful and wise in the teachings of their cultures. April was a respected elder in her community. I knew they were going to be at the circle that night so I quelled my anxiety with the thought of their help and support.

The group was led by a medicine woman, Sieras, from Manitoulin Island in northern Ontario. She instructed us in the teachings and led us in the ceremony and ritual that was the basis for healing and living in the native tradition. That night I learned the ceremonies of smudging, to clear the space and our bodies of any negative energy from outside the circle. Lighting a wand of dried sage, Sieras brushed the smoke into our bodies with her eagle feather. She then passed the smudge to the last person so that she also could be cleansed. I watched what each woman did very closely so that I would not make a mistake and perhaps offend someone.

Sieras opened the circle with a prayer that included an invitation to the spirit world to be present and a thanksgiving for all our ancestors and those beings that watch over us and walk with us on this journey. We were invited to pray, to add what we felt inspired to say, after her prayer was completed. Each woman had brought an offering that she then placed in the center of the circle: an offering to the spirits of the ancestors and thanks for their presence and energy in this sacred circle.

Sieras spoke of the talking stick, a wooden stick decorated with eagle feathers and beads that had been made for this group by another circle in the north. It rested in the middle of the circle and, as each of us felt prompted to say something, we would reach for the stick and hold it. We kept the stick for as long as we were inspired to speak and others could not interrupt or offer advice. It was very important to speak from our heart in this sacred space. The qualities of respect and honor for life, for each other, for our hearts were almost tangible within that space.

In the circle I began to learn the art of detachment. Rather than getting emotionally involved in what other people were saying, I tried to just observe them, who they were and the words they were sharing. The circle would teach me this principle over and over: every time I was disappointed that April wasn't there or impatient because we were late starting, or annoyed because I wanted a different teaching than the one Sieras was covering, or tired when someone was talking on and on and I wanted it to be over. Patience, acceptance, and a willingness to allow Spirit to work magic were the lessons of these circles for me. I found my psychic abilities opening even further as I practised the art of detachment. Life became a little easier.

"Spirit" was the word I had chosen to describe the power often referred to as God. It provided some psychological distance from the God of my childhood, the God of formal religion. It was a term that I found to be more descriptive of the loving spiritual presence I desired in my life. Spirit was also able to encompass the various teachings I was drawn to, whether Native American, Buddhist or Tibetan shamanism. It was my general term for the "God in all things." As my friend Victoria, an Ojibwa woman from Thunder Bay in Ontario, frequently reminded me, "It's all the same Light, just a different lamp."

Detachment allowed my own energy to flow rather than getting caught up in another's. It provided psychic distance so that I could begin to distinguish between others and myself on a psychic and energetic level. As a result I was less afraid of getting overwhelmed and drained by another person's story. I could open more to receive impressions and senses of the energies around me.

I could see that something occurred in that circle of women. Our energies came together in the center more strongly than in any one of us alone, as if to create space that held new form, the "oneness" of our shared experience.

Space began to fascinate me: the space held by a circle, the space of a room, the space on the tundra, the momentary space between our thoughts, and the space between our actions. What was held in that space? What could I learn from those spaces?

Sieras' suggestion that we go out to her cabin for a weekend retreat was greeted with a great deal of enthusiasm. The day was cool and cloudy as I drove out to Prelude Lake, 30 miles from Yellowknife, and it looked like it would be a damp and grey weekend for the retreat. As it was, much of the work that we did took place inside the cabin. Saturday was spent in teaching and preparing a "giveaway" and in shared laughter and tears. I had reflected deeply on the beliefs, attitudes and people that I needed to give away, release from my life, so that an open space would be created which would draw in the new. I had also pondered on the need for change and what I now wanted to attract into my life. I had a dream that night of a ceremony of creation at the edge of a lake where I found a crescent-shaped rock to hold the sage that I would use for smudging.

Sunday morning I walked alone around the lake, wanting to do a private ceremony of thanks and to honor my dream. I came to a rock outcropping which jutted into the lake, and as I looked down, I saw the crescent-shaped rock of my dream lying on the ground. I knelt down to begin preparing for the ceremony, the first ritual I had done like this. With matches in hand I tried to light the sage that I had placed on the rock. It wouldn't light.

I stopped and asked for help and insight about what I was doing wrong. As I sat at the edge of the lake, quiet in meditation, a large malamute walked out from the forest onto the rock outcrop. Her startling, ice-blue eyes held mine entranced, as she stood outlined against the lake. I was reminded strongly of the wolf that I had known in Arctic Alaska and of Tuktu. I knew I had no need to fear her.

She walked back to the path and lay down, effectively blocking access to the outcrop by anyone else. I gave her a thank you and found that the sage lit immediately. She lay there watching me, her brilliant eyes following my every move as I prayed and asked for guidance in the changes that were coming in my future. The wind blew from each of the four directions in a clockwise manner during this ceremony: from the north, the home of the ancestors, then east, south, west, and back to north, fanning the sage gently and keeping it alight. I ended the

The rocky lakeshore where Dyan did her ceremony of thanks.

ceremony with thanks and placed an offering of corn and tobacco at the base of the grandfather fir tree which grew at the edge of the rock.

I gathered up my sage and matches and the rock that I had dreamed about and started to walk back to the cabin. The malamute walked with me along the edge of the lake up to the porch of the cabin, apparently intent on insuring my safe return. She was my sacred witness that day. I asked Sieras about her when I returned and she knew of no dog like that anywhere around this cabin, so isolated in the northern boreal forest. I had no doubt as to the presence of Spirit that day.

DREAMS

Dreams have always been powerful teachers in my psychic experience. These are the times that my guides can appear and bring graphic insights and messages to help in my search. Since they first appeared to guide me to the Learning Place, these spirits have come in many of my dreams through the years.

There are two kinds of dreams: processing dreams, which review and relive the events of the day, and prophetic dreams. The latter, which take daily events a few steps further, often held answers or information for the resolution of problems that I was encountering in my daily life.

In Yellowknife, one autumn Saturday, I received a frantic, hysterical phone call from a close friend. It took a few minutes to find out what had happened. She and her three children, aged seven, five and one, had been thrown out of their house by her husband. She had nowhere to go and asked if she could stay with me. I had a spare room and was pleased that I could offer her a place of refuge. She brought many more people with her, however, over the course of the two months she stayed with me. My normally quiet house turned into what seemed like a train station with her and her children, her lover and his children and their respective spouses.

I would go to sleep at night asking for help and courage to follow a path of unconditional love, for understanding and forgiveness of the chaos that my friend had brought into my life. My pleas were answered with profound insight and a way to provide a sense of support and forgiveness for myself.

During a dream one night in that tumultuous time, I found myself standing in a room that seemed to be made completely of marble: the walls, floor and ceiling. These surfaces glowed with a golden light shining through the marble, illuminating the interior. Three beings, angels perhaps, sat at one end behind a table or dais; I was standing in the middle in front of them. There were no apparent entrances or windows, no source of light, yet the room was filled with a bright golden hue. After some discussion about how I was living my life and some indications where I could do better, it became apparent that I was in front of a tribunal of sorts, my High Council. This is a group of spirits that come together just prior to the birth of each person to help us in our lives. They serve as our guides, our guardian angels.

All of a sudden I sensed this message: "We want you to know what awaits you after death, so that you may know the outcome of your journey on Earth." With that, an archway opened on my right and I saw a blazing white light surrounding a tall figure at the end of a corridor.

I began to walk toward the opening, compelled by the light without knowing why, but I was told to wait. As the light reached out through the corridor, it touched me and I felt a sense of love more powerful than any I'd felt before. It was pure, unconditional and exquisite. It was absolute. It washed over me like an oceanic wave of tingling energy, flowing through each cell in my body. "You will remember when you awaken, so that you will know that this was real; this was more than just a dream."

As I opened my eyes in the morning, I remembered, and felt the energy of that love again. This continued for the next 20 minutes while the memory of "home" awakened by the dream came into my awareness. It was a memory more ancient than this lifetime, the home of my origin, and with it came an awareness of the desire of the ancient ones for all of us to return.

This was an important dream to me. My life and my house were filled with chaos and struggle. To know that this kind of love and peace awaited me gave me hope for the future and enabled me to carry on.

About three weeks later, during a particularly traumatic time when the wife of my friend's lover turned up at my front door and my living room was filled with the energies of children, estranged spouses and the unrepentant couple, I dreamed again of my guide with the deep brown eyes. He was standing in a void, a blue space so infinite there was no form and no ending, like the depth of the tranquil ocean water reflecting the summer sky.

He clearly asked what I most desired, and in my exhaustion from all that was going on in my life and the lives of those around me, I replied without hesitation, "Eternal love." It was an intriguing and unexpected desire, but why ask for something small?

Upon receiving that reply, he gestured for me to look to my right. Through the blueness, I saw the light being that I had seen in the previous dream. Blazing with an intense brilliance like an arc-welding flame, which was nevertheless peculiarly soothing to my eyes, the figure held out a hand to me and, without hesitation, I walked into the transparent liquid light.

The sense of merging, of becoming that light, of being that light and yet not losing my sense of identity was incredible. I lost a sense of who I thought I was, my personality perhaps, and became a pure light spirit. Again, I felt the energy of pure, unconditional love, so tangible I could drink of its sweetness. The vibration of complete and total acceptance reached through my body, its cells, into my heart and beyond, to the very essence of who I was, the core of my being.

When I awoke the next morning, I could not mistake the waves of energy washing over me. I lay in bed, luxuriating in the exquisite sense of love and acceptance, unconditionally available and given. That ocean of love bathed me, softened me, gently rocked me with its ebb and flow until all doubt, all separation was washed away. The ecstatic vibration continued to fill me, to wash through me for the next four days. I felt truly blessed with a deep sense of gratitude.

That energy slowly receded and I felt it infrequently through the next weeks. This powerful experience, this total body awareness of the love that awaits us, taught me that we can find love here on Earth when we are living our truth and remaining focussed on the highest good for all.

I think of those dreams often in times of stress and wonder if there was a purpose that I needed to pursue. Perhaps I should have taken my soapbox to the street corner and proclaimed the magnitude of the love that awaits us when we return home. I was unsure of what to do and so told only a few people. I know that I lost all fear of death through those dreams; it is a celebration to be born into that light.

SERENDIPITY

Yellowknife continued to be a place where the subtle energies of people and places were in clear evidence. Living there was always an adventure. My friends and I would get our tarot cards read, dance the winter nights away and plan canoeing and kayaking expeditions under the midnight summer sun.

Much of my time and energy was taken up by my two growing children, aged five and eight, and my government job. After my marriage ended, being a single parent in the north, this land of contrasts, often stretched me to my limit.

With the months of icy cold and dark days, I would travel south to find the sun at mid-winter. I was drawn to the Yucatan region of Mexico to explore the Mayan ruins of the area. These times re-awakened my desire to know more about psychic phenomena and experiences of unusual energy.

One such experience took place at Tulum. This is a walled Mayan city on the coast near Cancun. Only one gateway exists through the wall and as soon as I set foot on the other side, into the city area, the world took on a different quality. The energy was lighter, clearer, more pristine. My body felt unusual there and I began to remember sights and sounds from ancient times: of masks and headdresses, of people gathering together, of ceremonies occurring on the tops of the pyramids. I dismissed these impressions as vague memories from my university courses in anthropology, yet I wondered about the intense color of the pictures and the fine details of the masks. Could my memory of a university course from 15 years ago really be that vivid?

Curious and perplexed, I wasn't sure how I was receiving these impressions, yet they were as plain as day and very familiar. I spoke with the tour guide about the rituals and ceremonies and they seemed to be consistent with what anthropologists and archaeologists had discovered.

In the following years, I met other women by chance who had had nearly identical experiences. Tulum is believed to be a sacred area for the Mayas, the place where their holy leaders spent time in retreat, a power spot with unusual energy.

The Gulf Islands of British Columbia are a magical place closer to home, islands filled with petroglyphs and power spots. Bed-and-breakfast houses and retreat centers dot the islands and with the wonderful summer weather, they serve as a mecca for seekers from all over the world.

In the spring of 1991 I received an ad for a workshop called Adventures in Consciousness. In my new job as a policy advisor to the cabinet of the Northwest Territories government, I found intuition to be valuable in designing policy and information packages for the native government, and the style of intuitive decision-making mentioned in the workshop ad would build my skill.

There are crossroads in every life journey where a single decision, a single yes or no, will change a life forever. With one such decision, to attend this workshop, my life and that of my family moved onto an unexpected path.

Taking the train to Nanaimo on the east coast of Vancouver Island was a ride through hills and small towns and evergreen forests painted with the dappled light of that early August afternoon. It was so calming that I felt that I could leave the busyness of my life behind for the next week. Knowing that August was always a pivotal month in the seasons of my year, I wondered what this one might hold. August was the month before my birthday and it seemed that major life changes would happen then, as if to set my life up for the lessons of the next year. Whether it was divorce, marriage, illness or job change, something significant had happened in August for the past 15 years.

After a brief ferry ride from Nanaimo to Gabriola Island, I registered at the resort and retreat center where the workshop was to be held, then went to my room to meet my roommates for the week. I was sharing a room with two women from different parts of the country and we struck up a conversation to introduce ourselves as we unpacked. Once settled, I wandered through the grounds towards the beach. Nestled right at the ocean's edge, the land was bursting with the full bloom of summer flowers and the scent of cedar and ocean spray.

I was thrilled to be there; the sun and the ocean felt healing to my spirit after the dryness and cold of the north. Exploring the strange caverns and crevices that the waves had sculpted over centuries in the soft sandstone along that beach reminded me of how the ocean currents of our lives sculpt and shape the very essence of who we are.

Twenty-two of us gathered that Sunday evening in the meeting room to share who we were and what had led us to this workshop. I was astonished to find that Malcolm, the man seated next to me, knew my co-workers and supervisor in Yellowknife, since workshops like these were usually anonymous, everyone being strangers. This was a serendipitous beginning to what was supposed to be a fairly ordinary workshop.

Serendipity is a chance meeting with an unlikely outcome — it is the energy for making fortunate discoveries seemingly by accident. Often, the results direct one's life onto a completely new course.

Each morning after breakfast at the edge of the ocean, I walked with anticipation to the workshop room. We began slowly with some guided visualization, to establish a safe place on the inner planes, to learn techniques for clearing, and to begin our introduction to trance states. We all have an inner world, an inner landscape, much like our external world. It is in this imaginary world, so fluid and dynamic, that we visualize success or failure, visualize how our day will unfold. It is here that athletes begin the process of seeing themselves as winners. We can create a rich inner life here, much like the mystics of ancient times.

We worked with goal-setting in trance for the first day or two and then moved on to more interesting material. We did all of the work in trance, a way to consciously gain access to the imagery of the right brain. Lee, a university professor and the leader of this workshop, would give us what he called "left-brain crunchies," to keep the linear, analytical part of our minds busy, while we worked with our creative side. This was an excellent idea, since otherwise our left-brain analysis becomes distracting. Balance again, and so important for this exploration.

Lee led us, as a trail guide would, along the pathway from the developed and organized pastures of the valley bottom of everyday life and thinking to the expanded vision at the peak of the mountain where new, previously unseen worlds lie waiting to be beheld.

The hiking boots we wore, metaphorically speaking, were curiosity, commitment and allowing events to happen. If we tried too hard, too seriously, the process became blocked, the hike exhausting. We learned, while trying to bend spoons with our minds, that a playful attitude and lighthearted inquiry into this serious endeavor provided the type of energy needed.

Imagination worked wonders. To keep Lee from pulling my thumb and forefinger apart, all I needed to do was imagine my fingers forming a brass ring, rather than try to hold them together. It was effortless and, as Lee said over and over, when it's effortless you know you've got it right.

After many guided visualizations to build our inner landscape, with safe gardens, healing pools, golden screens for clearing and cleansing waterfalls, and meeting our spirit advisors and power animals, Lee began to provide us with opportunities to apply the skills that we were developing.

My power animals, the grizzly bear and the hummingbird, were with me, as well as a new guide, a beautiful Native woman in a feathered headdress and tanned skin clothes. They accompanied me on my trance journeys that week.

One exercise was to explore a skill called psychometry where an object is "read" to obtain information and impressions about the owner; Lee gave each of us an object, like a key, and asked us to locate the person in the room to whom it belonged and where it was used. Holding a ballpoint pen in my hand, I went into a light trance and tried to match up the energy of the pen with the energy of an individual in the room.

"Ah, Penny," I thought, "it's a match." But where did she use it? Slowly, I could see a desk, not unusual given that it was a pen; however, this desk was surrounded by stacks of books and filing cabinets. Certainly not at her home, I thought.

I walked over to Penny and asked her if the pen was hers. "Yes," she replied, smiling encouragingly.

"Do you use it at your desk where you work? And do you work in a library or bookstore?" I asked hesitatingly.

"Why, yes," she responded enthusiastically. "You're right."

I was quite astonished. Even though I knew it was possible, I still didn't believe it.

Sitting in pairs one afternoon, we each tuned in to our partner's home. This was a great exercise because we received immediate feedback as we described what we could see about the other person's home. As we sat I began to get a sense of Ann's house and a faint picture of it but I couldn't see the front door. In the living room I could see a large picture window with the drapes drawn. Finally I asked her about this. She said she always opened the drapes in her house, yet she was a private and very quiet person, reluctant to let anyone get too close or to expose much of herself to the outside world. This was very intriguing to me, the mixing of physical and emotional aspects in a single psychic picture. The home that I saw reflected her emotional expression as much as it did the physical structure of her house.

During an exercise in automatic writing, in which you write in free association while in trance, I began writing and soon had the feeling that my hand was being guided by another's thoughts. She wrote that her name was Allandra and that she had lived in the Balkans during the revolution. She told of being married and then, when the revolution came, of having to hide with the children in the hills. I was intrigued by her story and the speed of my writing. Automatic writing can become channeling, when we experience the thoughts and story of another being. Whether this is a spirit or angel, or whether the channel has tapped into the mass consciousness, depends on your frame of reference and belief system. This was a gentler presence than one that had appeared in an earlier experience with channeling.

The staff at the resort were friendly and gracious, the food well prepared and satisfying. Staying at the ocean's edge in a cabin among towering cedar trees provided a sanctuary, a haven, from the hectic pace of the daily world. Days were spent indoors in session. Late afternoons and evenings we walked the rocky shores of the ocean, watching the eagles dive for fish and the seals hauled up on the warm rocks, feeling the soothing rhythm of the waves and the serenity of the setting sun.

For one morning exercise, Lee gave us the latitude and longitude of a location somewhere in the world, and asked us to draw a picture of what we could see there. This was our first exercise in remote viewing. Not knowing the location of this point on the globe made it all the more mysterious. We went into light trance, as we had been taught, and began to sketch the picture that came to mind.

Seeing a series of broken columns and semi-circular benches, I began to sketch them on my paper. As I was sketching I could also see a white church beside the ocean; however, it didn't fit with the columns and benches. I struggled for quite a while to fit the two images together into some kind of coherent picture, but was unable to.

After the viewing time was over, we compared what we had seen. The location referred to was the amphitheater at Delphi in Greece, the place of the Greek oracle, with many broken and fallen Greek columns and semi-circular seating around the amphitheater. Everyone had managed to sketch images or impressions of the columns and amphitheater.

Pleased that I had been able to see this, I wondered about the white church and asked Lee where that might fit in. He was quite surprised and said that as we had been doing the exercise, he had been thinking of the church in Greece where his wife and he had married — a white church by the ocean.

Lee had set up what he called "dream teams" at the beginning of the week, groups of three people who would go to sleep with the intention of meeting at a certain place at 4:00 AM in their dreams. This was to help us awaken in our dream state, which is known as lucid dreaming or conscious dreaming. Malcolm, Lena, one of my roommates, and I were part of a team and, try as I might, I never made it to the lamp standard on the driveway at 4:00 AM.

As the week progressed, Malcolm and I spent more and more time together. It turned out that he was a forester with an M.Sc. practising wildlife biology and I was an ecologist with an M.Sc. practising wildlife biology; that during the 1970s we had each had an orange Volkswagen Beetle and a Siamese cat named Blue (I could hardly believe it); that I had lived on Arbutus Street and moved to Madrona and Malcolm had lived on Madrona and moved to Arbutus Street; that we both loved Crispy Crunch chocolate bars and sailing; and that at the moment I lived in Yellowknife and Malcolm lived at Yellowpoint. These were too many coincidences even for me. I kept asking myself what was the probability of encountering someone with so many similarities. It seemed as though we had been living parallel lives on separate planes of existence up to this point.

One day we practised health reading, an advanced kind of remote viewing. Given the initials G.S. and the location of Richmond, B.C., I was to try to give an assessment of this individual's health. With only the initials and location, the reader would go into trance and make contact, then begin to receive impressions and sometimes pictures of the person's health and well-being.

Lee had instructed us, before we left home, to ask a friend who had health concerns if they were willing to participate in this exercise and to be open psychically. He kept reminding us of the importance of having permission before doing any psychic readings involving another person. I had asked my friend Victoria if she would participate and she had agreed.

As I went into trance my mind was flooded with pictures. I could see an apartment and the furniture in it. I could see an energy form of brilliant red in the shape of a human body coming toward me and I had the impression of someone saying with a kind of chuckle, "So she did arrange it ...." I described the apartment's furniture and layout. Ann, the friend of G.S., confirmed that I was viewing the correct place.

I could see bones that were broken and having trouble mending. I could see that this body was walking, but had its hands out holding onto some kind of support, like a walker. I could see a dark and tumbling space where the stomach should be. I got a sense of the Pillsbury Doughboy, all white, soft and squishy, then the sense of a man driven to exercise as a desperate way to firm up his body and strengthen his muscles.

Again, I was astonished at this information flowing into my mind, as pictures complete with sound and feeling. I didn't know how to control or direct the information, or stop the flood once it started.

As I relayed all this, I was wondering where it was coming from and if any of it was accurate. Ann knew G.S. and said a yes or no to the information I was communicating. Almost all of it was accurate. I had a sense of coming home in some way, to myself.

G.S. had been in a motorcycle accident and had been quite badly injured. His bones were slow to knit, and the doctor at the workshop stated that the drugs he was taking would cause a great deal of stomach discomfort. As for the Pillsbury Doughboy, Ann said that he did seem driven to long workouts for several days a week and, as he appeared fit and trim, she never understood why, so the information that he saw himself as the Pillsbury Doughboy made sense of some apparently extreme behavior.

Lee then asked me to go inside the body of G.S. and look for problem areas, starting at his head and moving down to his feet.

The only thing that I could see was a very waxy, yellow spot the size of a dime on the surface of his brain. The doctor said that this could have resulted from a head injury which rendered G.S. unconscious after the accident. When I described the broken bones and surrounding tissue, the doctor again corroborated the accuracy of the information.

This was wild! I would never have believed it if I had been told at the beginning of the week that this kind of remote viewing was possible. And the best part was that everyone in the workshop was successful at locating the person with the initials and location, describing accurately the health conditions of the candidate. The person who read Victoria had picked up her gall bladder disease exactly.

The implications of this were astounding: to be able to travel anywhere in the known world at any time, encountering whatever energies happened to be there. I wanted to know more, and yet the prospect alarmed me. What were the dangers, the pitfalls? Could I get lost and be unable to get home?

During the week, Malcolm and I had formed a deep, caring connection psychically. We had walked parallel paths, in many respects, and we talked about bridging those paths through working together and laughing together. As the workshop drew to a close, we agreed to stay in touch and to visit remotely between Yellowknife and Yellowpoint, to continue our explorations and adventures as a dream team.

I returned home to my children and my job, but my perception of reality had changed so significantly that I was unable to live my life in the ordinary way, as I had lived it before. That life was too small and I physically hurt as I tried to bend myself back into the old routines and responses. I was thankful that I could call Malcolm and connect with someone who had also experienced this; he was a touchstone and a ground to confirm the authenticity of that workshop.

During the workshop we had practised and tried different exercises designed to release our psychic abilities and to have successful outcomes with these new skills. I always told myself that everyone else was psychic, but not me; at least that's what I

65

had decided when I was a teenager, until this workshop. I could no longer deny my experiences there, nor the fact that I had been using many of these methods unconsciously for most of my life. I became aware of seeing the world from another perspective — a way based on psychic reading and knowing — the gateway into realms of subtle energy in non-ordinary reality.

The effects permeated every aspect of my life. At work, when I heard someone wonder about how their children were doing that afternoon, or when someone was wondering if the grocery store had a certain item, I was tempted to say, "Well, just go and look," meaning remote viewing. I had a new and expanded sense of what was possible.

In truth, once we have the awareness, there is no going back — ever. Once our consciousness has expanded, we are changed — forever.

CHAPTER FIVE

MAJOR MOVES

OVER DISTANCE

MALCOLM AND I talked on the phone every day, sharing our insights and the new reality we were sensing since the workshop. We used to set up a time and place to meet psychically, usually at 4:00 AM, although sometimes in the early evening. The first time I tried to visit Malcolm I went down at bedtime to say goodnight. I could see him lying in bed reading a sailing magazine, the lamp on a small bedside table beside his pillow. I immediately called him to see what he was doing.

"Just here lying in bed reading *Pacific Yachting* and thinking of you," he replied to my excited questions. "Good work," he said, after I described what I could see.

I visited again the next morning, but got quite confused by bars or beams forming a triangular space somewhere in his cabin. I couldn't describe it well enough for Malcolm to identify it; however, the first time I walked into his cabin I knew exactly where I had been — up in the far corner of his ceiling, where the rafters met to form a triangle.

One night, we decided to go sailing together after dinner; I was to join Malcolm remotely at his boat in Maple Bay. I "went" down to the sailboat and found it tied up at the dock with the engine still warm. When I phoned later that evening, he said he had waited for me but had got cold, so he went back to the dock and drove home. I had missed our sail.

Malcolm also came up to visit me, although one night I didn't sense him. When he called on the phone he asked me if I had a very small room, painted blue and seemingly filled to the ceiling with so many toys he couldn't find the way out. He had ended up in my son's bedroom closet, painted blue and filled with toys! We had quite a giggle about his landing in that closet and his sense of direction in non-ordinary reality.

Curious about where this relationship was leading, I flew down to Yellowpoint Lodge to meet Malcolm and explore our growing and joyous connection. And so I found myself in meditation one crisp fall morning, seeking answers to the most monumental questions of my life: should I quit my job, leave my community and move 3,000 miles to be with Malcolm and build a new life with him?

As I began to journey, seeking my guide, desert images rose in my mind's eye. She would be there waiting. I began to sense that she was a medicine woman from the times when Chaco Canyon in New Mexico was occupied by Native Americans. I could see the red desert hills, the sagebrush and cactus, the sand beneath my feet. She had first come as a new guide for me during the workshop on Gabriola and I was glad to see her again. She was much gentler than my other guides and I was glad to have a feminine companion during my travels in other realms.

While I followed her through the desert she would call my attention to tiny plants that I had not noticed. "This one is good for bites," she would instruct, "this one to help with pain." She moved swiftly around the land, always alone and sure of her kinship there. Often, gazing into the air that shimmered with the heat and the reflected desert floor, she seemed to be sensing an energy that I was unaware of.

"You need to follow me now," she said as we walked through narrow canyons and gullies. She taught with love, and about love; love for the land and the rocks, for the plants and animals that lived on this earth.

Filled with respect and caring for all that is, she opened me to an experience of the sacred that lies wherever we look, whether it is within ourselves or the surrounding environment. In these meditations when Medicine Woman, as I called her, was my guide I would follow willingly; there was so much to learn and she was such a wise woman. She would point to the coyote running along the ridge tops and tell me the story of the trickster, the energy that is constantly challenging our beliefs about what we are anticipating. Just as we think we've got life all figured out, Coyote could turn up with the unexpected trick which shakes our fondly held ideas about reality.

"Bring Coyote into your medicine bundle, so that you can laugh at his tricks when he shows up in your life, rather than feeling frustrated and unaware," she said. This would turn out to be directly relevant to my time with Malcolm.

"And look at a hummingbird, come to bring joy into this land that so many people think is empty. Watch Hummingbird, the only bird that can fly backwards and hover in one spot, choosing which way she will dart next. Learn from Hummingbird the story of how to walk out of time's clothing into ecstasy and the need for all beings to be free to fly in their own way. Hummingbird medicine will help you to move in and out of the dark, and the light, in your journey. Carry her with you, that you might consider and know the joy held by that small being, the joy that often eludes humankind."

She had studied with the wise ones that live with the Spirit of the Desert, and although she appeared in my meditations, she was not yet a spirit in her world. The desert was entrancing that day, warm and gentle with many tiny plants and animals full of curiosity. We traveled a long way, along arroyo edges much like the ocean edge on which I sat.

While I didn't really understand all she taught, I paid attention and hoped that when the time came I would know what to do. The next few years would teach me the truth of Hummingbird, for when they are captive and caged, a hummingbird will die with longing for freedom, as I would almost die over the next five years.

I came slowly out of the meditation, my stomach grumbling with hunger and nudging me back toward lunch at the lodge. As I stood up, I looked out over the ocean, wondering what Medicine Woman was sensing when she scanned the desert, what energy was there in the far vistas, what energy trail she was following. I wondered about her teachings and how they would provide answers to the questions that I was asking. As usual, the answers were more subtle than direct, requiring interpretation and insight to find the truth held within the direct experience.

Then as I began to walk back to the lodge, I looked down at my feet following the path along the grassy meadow and realized that they were also walking a canyon's red path through the desert. This was double vision in a way that I had not experienced before. The two images were superimposed and transparent, so that I was looking through the desert floor to the grass underneath my feet. Even though I was fully conscious, I knew that I was walking in both realms at the same time — and attempting not to trip in either!

In keeping with radical decisions, that weekend Malcolm and I decided to plan a life together: I would move to Yellowpoint the following spring and then, in August, Malcolm and my sons and I would move to Victoria.

Until the time that we could be together we practised remote viewing and spent hours talking on the telephone. I would often be lying in bed, just before falling asleep, and feel his energy flop down on the bed beside me. Malcolm was very skilled in energy work, and gifted psychically, and when I asked him the following morning, he would usually be able to give me a time when he traveled up to visit and curl up in bed. It was most often at the time I felt him arrive.

The immediate confirmation, between us, of our remote viewing and travel experiences was an essential part of our growing psychic abilities. Without that, doubt can creep in because you're never really sure that it's not just your imagination, at first.

One of the things that I did to include my sons in this new expanded awareness, and in the idea of creating reality, was to get them to help me in manifesting parking places. It became a great game. When we left home we would decide where we wanted the parking space to be and then expand a thread of consciousness out to touch it. We felt a great sense of accomplishment when the space was there, right where we had asked for it. As the winter progressed, we grew quite proficient at creating parking spaces. I was thankful that Devin and Aiden were open to these experiences and to the possibility of moving to Victoria.

Wanting to get an idea of the future I began a series of trances in the fall, asking the question: "Which house could we buy when we go house hunting in the Mount Tolmie area, during the third week of April?" We knew that we would be looking then, after I had moved down to Yellowpoint. This was great fun, playing in non-ordinary reality, unaware of any dangers that might be present there, like two kids visiting a new fairground. One evening in October I traveled remotely to Victoria, to the Mount Tolmie area, and ahead to April of the next year, to see what houses would be available to purchase in that third week.

I began to see a small grey stucco house with a front porch. The porch was open and to one side of the front door. There was a window on the other side. It was an old style of house, built in the 1940s. The yard was full of trees and had a long driveway leading beside the house. The image was indistinct at first and sharpened in clarity as I focussed more on the question. I had no idea where it was located in Victoria, although I assumed it was around Mount Tolmie. Remotely, I looked at it for several nights, hoping to gather more details so that I would be able to find it.

When I went down to Victoria for Christmas, Malcolm and I drove around the area in an attempt to find the house I had seen. As we were coming up a side street, there it was, right in

71

front of us, glowing brightly as if it was under a spotlight, which happens for me when there is a match between a psychic image and a physical one: the colors are intensified in other realms, almost neon in their brightness. I had discovered that when I saw something during trance and then saw it again in the physical realm, it would glow with amazing brightness, a signal that it had a heightened or charged energy.

"There it is!" I shouted, and pointed to the house. "But it's not right — there's no porch." The house I had seen clearly had a porch. Yet this one glowed, a sure sign that it was the one I had looked at. There were lots of trees, the driveway running beside the house, and grey stucco.

We laughed, and talked of how we would get the people to sell it to us in April. Would we walk up to the door and ask them to move? Would we just let them know that we were interested in buying it? We planned all sorts of ways to persuade the people to sell it, not really trusting that it would be for sale in April.

When I came down in February we found another house that we both loved and put in an offer. All thought of the third week in April and the house at the bottom of the hill were forgotten in the excitement. In our impatience we couldn't wait for the house I had seen to come on the market. Perhaps we didn't trust that it would happen; perhaps we didn't really trust that it would be there for us. It seemed so improbable.

During that third week in April, after I had left Yellowknife, we were driving along in Victoria, approaching the block of the glowing house.

"Oh my God, oh my God," Malcolm said in an astonished voice. "Look at that." I couldn't figure out what he was so excited about until I saw a sign on the front lawn of the grey stucco house, the large red letters spelling FOR SALE.

"Right on cue." I laughed and said, "Well, we wouldn't have had to knock on their door at all. We would only have needed to walk in and buy it."

We toured the house when the agent staged an open house the next weekend. As we were going through it we realized that it had been built with a porch that had been enclosed later.

My sight had been absolutely accurate in time, place and quality this time. It was the only house for sale in that area during the third week of April that year.

This was a good lesson for me about the possibility of the future. It is not fixed, and evolves as we make our choices and decisions each day. The house was going to be there for us if we were shopping for one in the third week of April, exactly as I had asked. However, we bought our house in February. That choice did not change the future regarding the availability of houses in the third week; it did, however, direct our future onto a very different pathway.

The critical question is about rightness, just like "right time." Is this the right house for us? Is this the right choice for our happiness?

As I looked ahead to my move south and our wedding and life together, I had no indication of what lay in store for me. As much as it's possible to see ahead, in a real sense, there is also a part of us that doesn't really want to see exactly what the future holds in store — the veil so often spoken of by mystics. Even if we have well-developed psychic abilities, perhaps each of us is here to learn particular lessons for our own growth and evolution, which, if we knew about them beforehand, might not hold such deep learning.

We see dimly through that veil, if at all. It takes commitment, courage, a strong sense of self-responsibility and great curiosity to want it removed entirely.

THE "T" WORDS: TRANSITION, TRANSFORMATION, TRUTH

It had been a hectic time, this leaving a life behind to begin anew. Six months of dismantling a household and a life I had built over ten years, to have the opportunity of a new and different world with the man I loved from the very core of my being, the kind of love that only comes once in a lifetime.

The last hurdle was to drive the thousands of miles from Yellowknife to Yellowpoint. The roads were good, though the trip would entail crossing the Mackenzie River on the still-frozen river over the ice bridge.

Remembering those days now, as I sit watching the hummingbirds drink nectar from the feeders at my cabin, I feel it all again. Awash with tears, I cried from fear over the step I was about to take, and from longing for the safety of Malcolm's arms sheltering me, and from the joyful anticipation of this new life unfolding. Amazed, I noticed that the release of tears looked the same whether they were filled with fear and grief or the joys of love.

I remember worrying for weeks about the ice bridge across the Mackenzie River melting before we could cross from the Northwest Territories into Alberta; I listened intently to the weather forecast every morning, praying for cold weather. This was the first and only time in the 11 years that I lived in the NWT that I prayed for cold weather. I had looked psychically to see if I would be turned back, but there was safe passage. Not trusting what I saw, I continued to worry.

April 3rd dawned with clear sky and much-appreciated low temperatures. After packing the last few plants in the car, we started off down the ice-packed highway toward Fort Rae, the first signpost on our journey south. Malcolm drove through that clear air towards the Pacific Ocean, three thousand miles away. My heart was flying home.

Chatting about life in general, and my life in the NWT, I shared stories with Malcolm as the car carried us along. After all those years, each curve held a story to recount. With thermoses of tea and cookies we began our journey together.

A couple of foxes darted across the road, the only wildlife we had seen along the desolate highway until we passed through Fort Providence, a "one gas station community" that hugs the shores of the river just north of the ice bridge.

Without warning a bull caribou burst from the snowy brush at the side of the road. I excitedly cried to Malcolm, "Your first caribou, and just before we leave; a spirit come to say goodbye." Malcolm was doing his best to watch the road, even though he was looking at the caribou.

Three females emerged, trailing behind the bull. Running onto the ice-covered highway, the bull galloped beside my car, close

74

enough to touch, for quite a stretch toward the bridge, a wild Arctic spirit come to wish us safe journey.

Yet, it was strange behavior, like a dog chasing a car. Was he trying to call me back — a warning — or was he providing an escort for the last few hundred feet to the river? Malcolm, as a biologist, was delighted at finally seeing some Arctic wildlife.

And then the frozen river appeared at the end of the road. An ice bridge is no more than a ploughed section of frozen river, the only marker being the place where the land ends and the river begins.

Leaving the past behind and stepping into the future — the metaphor of this threshold hadn't escaped me, from the wilderness of the Arctic landscape to the future of a tamed cityscape. This gateway was captured in the azure ice of that frozen river crossing where, at the center of the bridge, in the center of the river, the world was glassy smooth, cold, white and completely without definition; my red car was like a blood-red bullet shot through the ice fog that thickened the air.

At the center of that river there was much to remember, and I realized I could choose to focus on the loss of all that I had known, or on the beginning of all that I would come to know. I could sense myself at that fulcrum, unsure and uncertain, teetering in the balance. Where was my commitment, I wondered, where was my unshakable optimism that this was right? In that moment of realization I felt as featureless as the frozen river itself. Then, in the stark whiteness of that winter April afternoon, we emerged on the southern shore and headed down the ruler-straight roads of Alberta.

My experience had taught me that expanded states of awareness, like those gained through meditation or peak creative experiences, for example, bring greater depth to our perception of reality. This seemed to be a benefit in preparing for expanded and integrated psychic potential. But I wondered, is it really just a matter of perspective? How can we find truth in all that we perceive, with our prejudices, our judgments, our needs? I longed to return to the Learning Place and ask the myriad questions that were turning over and over in my mind.

In the hours of that long drive, I remembered snippets from books I had read over the years. Mystics say we can only see what we already believe exists, and in that our world becomes a self-fulfilling and self-limiting prophecy. We see that which reinforces the view that we already hold. Was I going to be able to create a new future with this gentle, loving man? Was I strong enough to let go of all my past habits and patterns? Only time would tell.

Lives have been lost, families torn apart because we could not, would not, see the world from another's perspective. Like witnesses to an accident, each person has a unique description, a view of what happened, and no two stories are the same. Malcolm and I shared many of these ideas during the long journey, hoping to find common ground, a common perspective. Devin and Aiden were spending the summer with their father in Yellowknife to give us an opportunity to spend time together alone before beginning our stepfamily.

The more I wondered about perspective and common ground, the more I remembered Angeline. Years before, this small, energetic woman had come into my life as part of a therapy group I was co-facilitating. I gained an understanding, through knowing her, of personal perspective and psychic sight quite unlike anything offered in Psychology 101.

Suffering from a dissociative disorder, she was insightful and courageous in wanting to integrate her separate selves to become whole. As we worked together she taught me a lot about perceiving reality. Each of her 13 selves saw the events of her life from a very different perspective. Some of her selves were male, some female, some young, some old, each with their own unique view of reality.

The question was how to build enough common ground among them to facilitate integration. During one of our sessions Angie, the evolving multidimensional personality of Angeline, recounted an incident during a performance evaluation at work. Kate (the prim and proper personality) felt that her boss had been fair in correcting her work as a secretary, Susan (who always cried) was crying because the boss had been abrupt when he commented on her work as a receptionist, Joe (who was the rebellious one) was angry because they shouldn't have to put up with this nonsense and the boss should just let her do her job as a clerk, and Ann, the only one who was psychic, kept saying, "I told you I could see this was going to happen, I told you," whereas Melissa (who was only five) was afraid of the big man and was trying to hide in the corner, and David (who was eight) figured that they should quit the job since the boss obviously didn't like them anyway. Tanya thought that sleeping with him might help. When asked about the details, they offered little consensus about what had happened during the evaluation, or even what the boss had been wearing.

The factor which created such insight for me was that all of these individuals, with their own unique views, feelings and behavior resided in the single body of a middle-aged woman. Was one right and the others wrong? I thought back to the Learning Center and my father's teachings about judging another's view of the world. Each response was based on a perspective appropriate to age, maturity, and experience. I wondered again how we ever got along in this world, and prayed that Malcolm and I, so similar and yet so very different, would be able to build the bridges and common ground that we would need.

Gazing at the dense boreal forest of northern Alberta, I wondered about many things in life, each stand of trees seeming to bring yet more questions about the nature of reality and perception. Stopping overnight in the small, back-country towns along the highway brought a sense of different energies, of unique livelihoods in each town. On the highway or not, in the forest or in the mountains, each place had a sense of its own presence. I wondered if the people in each town were shaped by the land in which they lived, much as I had been shaped by the Arctic. We traveled from the sub-Arctic to the west-coast rain-forest in a few days, the energies bringing a tangible experience of each locale. It was really an introspective trip, nestled in that red car, the color of love.

WHITE BEACH

Yellowpoint was a magical place that spring, after the frozen winter of the north. My experience had led me to believe that every single choice we make is right for our learning, even though some take us on to an experience of pain and struggle while others carry us to joy and peace. Like the yin/yang symbol of the ancient Chinese, life becomes a dynamic state of flow between polarities fueled by our decisions. Many of the decisions I made at this time would lead me into pain and struggle, rather than the joy and love that I dreamed awaited me with my move to the south, and to Malcolm.

The rose-colored world of new love had begun to fade just weeks after I moved to the coast. Feeling that I may have made a huge mistake, I was trying to decide whether to pack up and go home or see if Malcolm and I would become more relaxed as we spent more time together. We had already encountered serious problems between us, and my heart felt like it was breaking.

I was still in deep grief over my mother's death the week before I had left Yellowknife. Our mother-daughter relationship was poor at best and I had always said, from the time I left Vancouver 20 years before, that I would never move back to the coast as long as my mother was alive. I thought a lot about her passing, just seven days before I left the north to move to the coast. Do angry words and passionate intention really hold that much power, I wondered, as guilt and sorrow over her death rested in my heart. We had been working to heal our troubled relationship and I had been looking forward to being closer to her.

Yet perhaps those words spoken so long ago had held a force much stronger than I imagined. Was the power of the psychic realm somehow at play? That thought brought my reluctance to the surface again.

My mother had chosen her day to die, though, and in that I had to celebrate her passing. With clear intention and focus she had lain down on her bed that morning and when her nephew called in the afternoon she was close to death. The coroner was stumped, and when he called to say that he could find no cause of death — no drugs, no alcohol — I almost said to him, "It was her chosen day to die, and so she did." It's just mind over matter, as she always said.

I knew that returning to the natural world, to the ocean and the land, would bring peace to my heart. I spent countless hours that first summer roaming through the forest and along the water's edge, seeking clarity and some sense of what to do.

Walking along the ocean's shore just outside Malcolm's cabin, crushed clam and oyster shells crunching under my feet, I contemplated my life and direction. I stopped and gazed out onto the ocean, watching the sun glint off the wave tops, the brilliant blue sky a crisp backdrop to the deep-green, forested islands in Trincomali Channel.

Considering all this and trying desperately to see what lay ahead, my mind went completely still as I watched the waves brushing the sand along the beach, none of the usual chatter going on in my head. Moving into a trance state and empty of all thought, I was intensely aware of what was around me, absorbing it with all my senses — the taste of the ocean on the breeze, the smell of cedar boughs and rich earth, the cry of the gulls, the warm sun on my skin. In that transcendent energy, I felt a union with my environment so complete that "I" no longer existed.

However, what I wanted was more mundane than this elevated awareness. I wanted to see what would happen for us. I wanted my psychic sight to reveal my future.

As Brugh Joy notes in his book *Avalanche*, some situations "thin the veil that separates the conscious and the ordinary from the unconscious and the non-ordinary. ... I believe all psi (or psychic) experiences are products of transcendental states of consciousness, though not all transcendental states of consciousness produce psi experiences. There are transcendental or expanded states of awareness in which no unusual power or psychic phenomenon is evoked."[2]

For once I wanted the information that psychic wisdom could bring, and I wanted it desperately. I was so frantic to see ahead, so fearful of what I might see, that the whole process became blocked and I couldn't see anything.

TRANCE

Yellowpoint, that summer, was a time of trance: the trance of new love and failing love, the trance of dreams of hope and healing, and the trance of shamanic explorations into the psychic world. I began to follow the pathway of curiosity about other planes of existence and what lies beyond space and time. The summer was filled with sailboats and motorcycles, sunshine and warm salt air, breezes rustling the massive evergreens of the west coast as we lay safe in the cabin.

Malcolm and I had decided that I would take the next year off from work, to focus on building a healthy stepfamily and healing the blindness in my left eye that happened so long ago. I was hoping to regain normal vision.

That single year turned into several as the Pandora's box of healing consumed our lives. It was a time of impatience, frustration, triumph and compassion, with great and varied lessons for each of us. Reflecting back now, I remember long hours at the acupuncture clinic, severely restricted diets, and constant focus on the meaning of sight and vision in my life. I worked with the symbols in my dreams and used journaling in an attempt to gain access to hidden fears and beliefs which might have led to the blindness. I longed to be healed and healthy yet I seemed to be getting more and more ill.

There was little joy in those years of illness and healing. I remember that the struggle seemed never-ending, the stress overwhelming. I was unable to see any hope in my world and I despaired that I would ever find the light at the end of the tunnel. I was lost in the proverbial wilderness.

I searched for an explanation, some reason why I needed to experience these years of confusion and exhaustion, beyond my intention to heal my physical body and expand my psychic skills. I would cry to Spirit asking why, why was this happening, why couldn't I get out of bed, why couldn't I join my husband in our life together? I raged at Spirit, cried out my frustration and bewilderment.

As I opened up psychically, and entered this ocean of energy, I began experiencing emotions more and more strongly, both mine and others, as I had years before at the church door in Vancouver. The problem was that I was often overwhelmed by the energies of other people and left reeling in their wake, either energized or depressed. The more I opened, the more confusing it became, until I was unsure what belonged to whom. Since this experience can happen over distance, I wasn't necessarily in physical proximity to the individual who was broadcasting. I wanted to run to the closet, and never come out.

This is the point at which many people think they are going crazy and shut down completely to block the psychic opening. Crying for hours or feeling exhausted or angry for no apparent reason makes them feel insane. Their inside world of feeling, emotion, spirit, insight, empathy and connection is in the process of manifesting physically, and their world has truly turned inside out. Struggle with and resistance to this transformation hinder the process, and lengthen it.

Western medicine had no answers or suggestions to remedy what was happening. Consequently I turned to energy medicine, alternative healing. The more I opened the *chakras* or energy centers of my body and unblocked the energy meridians through acupuncture and other methods like massage, Reiki and reflexology, the more inexplicable feelings and information moved through me, leaving me shaken and paralyzed. I could be standing in the check-out at the supermarket and be overcome with feelings of anger or sadness, sometimes joy. Wondering why I was suddenly sad, I would notice that the feeling evaporated when the person beside me moved away. It was as if I had become a sponge for other people's emotional states.

Subtle energy can come from the earth, from man-made sources such as fluorescent lights and computers, from places and from people themselves. During this time I was not familiar enough with how to create energetic boundaries for protection, or energetic clearing and grounding. As I continued my healing work, I became super-sensitive to the energy around me and I found it exhausting, with no way to stop the roller-coaster ride. The energy systems of my body became so depleted that I was only able to stay up for one or two hours and could not manage the usual chores of running a home. I felt as though I was slowly dying.

Yet this time was also marked by triumph. I rejoiced at the periods of double vision that indicate that sight had returned to my blind eye, even though my brain was unable to integrate the images at first. I had an intense feeling of triumph as the color vision returned to my left eye. My world opened up again into the rainbow colors of the universe, and I would often burst out laughing with joy and delight in the beauty of this world. Malcolm shared the delight of this triumph; one step on the journey to health and full vision. My first pair of glasses that had a prescription for my left eye was a milestone, a triumph of bringing sight back.

Psychically, my vision was improving as well. I gained more clarity and connection with this ability, and actually began to enjoy its presence. With time, patience, and my determination to recover, my health slowly began to improve. Malcolm's generosity and steadfastness were commendable during this time, giving evidence of his strong conviction that we can heal our bodies completely, given the right conditions.

HUMMERS AND HEALING

Joy! Hummingbirds, those feisty, tiny little birds that will take on an eagle, were my talismans. Opening to everything, I was overwhelmed by shopping malls, and encouraged by hummingbirds. Every time I saw a hummingbird or felt the breeze from their wings, I would remember that they represented the energies of Joy, and the teaching of Medicine Woman.

One glorious summer evening I was standing at the sink washing the dishes when I heard a strange bird call. I turned and looked out the patio doors at the end of the kitchen. A hummingbird was hovering just on the other side of the doors. I saw him, and thought, without thinking, the feeder is empty. "Hold on," I said, "I'll fill it." He then flew away.

True to my word, I made some new syrup, since hummingbirds are seldom around on the coast in late August, and filled the feeder. As I was hanging it up, he rushed over and began drinking. I still had my hand on the feeder when he appeared. Slowly, ever so slowly, I withdrew my hand, so as not to startle him. When he had finished drinking, he hovered about five inches from my nose and made eye contact. For several moments, perhaps a minute, our gaze held. The essence of that bird was so present, so incredibly clear. And then he was gone.

Eye contact with a hummingbird was more than I had envisioned possible just a few years ago. Those years were very black. Filled with constant struggle, becoming exhausted from the least activity, unable to make the simplest things, like muffins, I despaired that my life would ever return to normal, that I would ever be able to dance again.

Life had become very precious after I was isolated from it for so long. Each rock, each cloud, each breath of wind was endowed with a vibrant energy that spoke to me of the inherent beauty and harmony of a world I had almost lost.

Joy was so close at that moment, in the warmth of the sun and a hummingbird's gaze. I saw the message: of finding joy in the simple, little things of life no matter what your circumstances.

INITIATION

Those first three years in Victoria were a time of initiation, a time of transformation down to the cellular level. Illness can be the beginning of a change of state, an expansion of ordinary consciousness that is often categorized as an initiatory experience. Thinking back on the years of exhaustion, I can see how that time was an intense wake-up call to me, to begin to live truly as who I am, rather than who I thought I was, or who I thought I should be, or who other people wanted me to be. Finally, I took to heart the words of the first counsel over the gateway to the temple at Delphi in Greece: "Know Thyself."

In June of 1994, I attended an eight-day Mayan Initiation workshop in Utah put on by Ariel Spilsbury, the author of *The Mayan Oracle*. It was a mythic workshop with ceremonies each night in which we would enact the archetypes of the Maya and encounter the vibratory energies of each of the Mayan glyphs.

On the last day before the drive to Salt Lake City to catch the plane back to Victoria, I was sitting in the hot tub with my soul sister WolfSong. She was a gentle and sweet person from the east coast of the United States. We had learned crystal singing, a vocal technique to shift energy in our bodies or in our physical world, and we wanted to practise together before we went our separate ways. The water was soothing and warm in the cool air of the forest around Ariel's house. We left the jets off so we could hear the birds' song and our own singing.

We went deeply into trance as we began to sing and slowly the tones became paramount. As I continued to sound the tones I could feel my connection extend down to the center of the earth itself, to the energy at the very core. As I drew that energy up into my body, the tone became deeper and more vibrant. I became aware of the sound vibrating in my body, as if it was a giant tuning fork that had been struck, and I was completely unaware of the need to take a breath. At one point I left my body, carried by the sound out into the world, as if on a wing. Continuing to tone, I merely floated over the landscape while still connected to the center at the core of the earth. It was quite wonderful to float gently over the hot tub and then down into Park City in the valley. I wasn't afraid any more.

Slowly, as the tone began to die, I opened my eyes and looked around at the trees and sunshine. I noticed that the hot tub was frothing and bubbling, tumbling with energy. I thought the jets must have been turned on by someone, but, as the tones drifted away, the tumultuous water stilled, until all was calm.

The vibration of our crystal song alone had stirred the water into those spirals and eddies. We looked at each other in awe, at the immensity of this expression of the power of energy and our new-found ability to call it forth. For a moment I wondered if this focussed sound, explored and trained, was the power used to build the pyramids.

JAGUAR ENERGY

The sacred energies of Bear and Hummingbird as my totems had supported me through those years of illness and unfolding. I could sense that a new animal energy was about to enter and I was curious about the form this would take. Our power animals change and shift along with our own growth and development, because they have so many messages for us.

I returned to Victoria energized from the Mayan workshop and ready to move out into the world. A new power animal would be helpful in guiding me into the new opportunities that awaited me. As always, my dreams were used as teachers, and I unexpectedly received a profound experience of this powerful energy at a direct and kinesthetic level.

My first encounter with Jaguar was one night as I was dreaming of the west-coast rainforest. I was walking down a cedar-lined path feeling curious about exploring deeper into the forest. It was dim and misty, the trees appearing suddenly out of the shadows and fog as I walked along the path. I became aware of eyes through the underbrush, watching me. "Uh, oh," I thought, a chill going down my spine. "Now what's going on here?" I was apprehensive about the possibility of this dream turning into a nightmare, and being pursued by some frightful form through the night. Not the kind of dream I enjoyed.

The feeling persisted as I walked farther along the path. Always curious, and by this time able to expand my psychic edges out further as a result of my meditation practices, I wanted to get a sense of what was behind those eyes. As I expanded psychically, the image of my body walking down the forest path came into focus. I was watching myself through the underbrush, and walking silently along beside me. However, now it wasn't a rainforest that I was walking though, but a dense jungle. A most interesting scene, I thought, walking through the jungle, watching myself walk through the rainforest. The appre-

85

hension I had felt previously disappeared, replaced by openness to this new experience.

That split image lasted only a moment as I turned my eyes to a new path that wandered along the jungle floor. I was so curious about this being that I had merged with that any thought or fear had long passed away. The elegant grace inherent in this body was at once apparent. It felt feline to me, as I imagined a cat's body might feel. The muscles were in fluid motion, and there were no extraneous thoughts in the mind: only those of the task at hand — walking and observing the jungle, sensing the vibrations of the air.

A stick cracked and the reaction was instantaneous — I was frozen for a split second as I waited for more information: whether this was friend, foe or dinner. No danger, and no dinner this time. It was evident that this creature was out hunting. I came eventually to a small water hole, the mirrored surface reflecting glints of moonlight in the dark jungle night. I approached the pool warily, alert for any sign of danger and, as I bent over to drink, I could see the piercing amber eyes reflected by the surface. Dimly lit was the black face of a jaguar, sometimes called panthers.

I could feel myself, some part of me, take a very deep breath and slowly exhale as I realized the amazing uniqueness of this experience. I knew I was dreaming, and knew also that on one level this dream was as real as my waking life. The grace of the animal was astounding. Even more so was the sense of oneness with the jungle and all it contained. There was no thought of separation between the jaguar and the jungle, only an instinctual response to the surroundings, an awareness of all senses simultaneously — much like the feeling of rightness when a decision or movement is based on our intuition. We, this creature and I, walked on to our favorite resting place and, after scanning the area with all senses, we lay down to rest. And with that I woke up in my bed. It was as if I had become a jaguar in this dream. The physical feelings were clear and intense and totally unlike my usual experience of moving in my physical body.

I joined with this being again the next night and then every night for two weeks, always by walking down that forest path and merging into the jungle. One night, as we were prowling down a faint path, a small creature ran in front of us. The response was lightning quick — and there was dinner. The kill was swift and the meat warm as we slowly devoured it. I thought about what I was observing and experiencing in this jungle, as a passive participant in this hunt, and considered the ways of our being in the world — our way of work and machines, of questioning and doubt, and the jaguar's way of complete confidence in being.

She was not without fear, as I found out one night. We were grooming our coat and it felt exquisitely sensuous to me to lick the skin of our shoulders, that rasping tongue massaging the skin and underlying muscles with smooth, repetitive motions. My shoulders in my cozy bed were tingling in response. Yet there was no sense of comparison in the mind of the jaguar. This grooming was as it should be, as it always had been, and was in some way comforting.

Resting and at peace after a good hunt and meal, her whole body tensed in response to a screech from a macaw. Her heart began to race and without another thought we were up on a high limb in the tree beside which we had been resting. And we were incredibly, absolutely still. Not even a whisker twitched. Absolute centered stillness with racing heart. Perhaps it was my heart that was racing in response to the shrill cry more than hers. We remained there until any sense of danger had passed and her body returned to resting as quickly as it had responded with arousal.

That leap was something I will remember for a long time. From relaxed to explosion in the blink of an eye — and we were up that tree. We humans carry that tension in our bodies all the time, in our modern world, but we have few trees to leap into for safety and nowhere to completely relax. Our reflexes get burned out until we are in a chronic state of excitation.

As I lay in my bed each night, I pondered the sensation of complete oneness with all things that I had experienced as a fully embodied part of that wild animal. Not only was I one with her, we were one with the world — the rocks, the jungle, the night sky. It was tangible and unquestionable.

There was no room in that creature for thought of Other. The closest I could come to it in my life was when I was pregnant and one with my babies or during those infrequent peak experiences watching a sunrise or paddling through whitewater in my kayak. But, more than that, this dream and others brought me an experience of the solid connection with the earth and all that exists on it: a transcendence of form and mind into unity, not as something that we inherently lack and have to strive for, but as a birthright to our being in this world.

INITIATIONS CONTINUE

During the next year, my energy began to return and my eyes continued healing. I felt as though my body had undergone a transformation, so that I no longer saw the world in the way I used to. I was getting out of the house more, and managing more of the household responsibilities.

Explorations into the realm of alternative medicine had led me to work with naturopathic doctors, homeopathy practitioners, bodyworkers, acupuncturists, shamans who practised soul retrieval and people who worked in the spiritual realms. I believed that in order to heal you have to work on all levels simultaneously so, while I focussed on the physical body, I also investigated emotional, mental and spiritual aspects of my loss of sight.

Even though my physical health was slowly improving, I was having trouble learning to "let go," to surrender. I struggled to let go of the way I thought things should be, to let go of the need to control — to control others, to control outcomes — to surrender my intense need for things to go my way. It was clear that this struggle was affecting my health and healing. Something in me, in my life, was crying out in the struggle, needing to change, to be healed, to be transformed. I prayed for direction, for insight.

Always curious, I began thinking of exploring the physical action of transformation and shamanic mystery. I felt strongly called to this way of being, having had so many Native American teachers and a Buddhist background. That call was getting louder.

As soon as I signed up for the Shamanic Initiation at a retreat on Cortes Island, my excitement started to grow. The facilitators, Richard and Donna, were shamans initiated in the traditions of the Huiochol in Mexico and the natives of Thailand. They also had formal scientific training. Donna was an M.D. and Richard had a Ph.D. in psychology. They had designed this workshop as a way to simulate the shamanic death experience of initiation for people who were unable to travel to remote places and undergo a traditional shamanic initiation. The intention was to create a psychic death in order to find freedom from the old ways — our old habits and beliefs.

Poems from Rumi would flash through my mind:

Begin as creation, become a creator.
Never wait at a barrier.
In this kitchen stocked with fresh food,
why sit content with a cup of warm water?[3]

The center offers many workshops during the summer months — from kayaking and basket weaving to dream explorations and deep ecology. Malcolm and I were staying in a cabin on the edge of the driftwood-covered beach along the ocean. Sun was pouring through the windows as I unpacked my clothes and lay down to try out the bed. The gentle lapping of the waves was a soothing welcome after the hectic journey from the city some six hours away. A hot tub sounded like a great idea before dinner. As I wound my way up the stone stairs to the main building, a snake slithered across my path. How incredibly wonderful, I thought, a beautiful gift and encouragement from Spirit.

Lying in the hot tub, overlooking the vast expanse of the ocean with towering evergreens at the back of the site, I pondered the message of the snake. A powerful medicine, Snake represents transmutation, the power of creation, sexuality, psychic energy, alchemy, and ascension (immortality): an appropriate symbol for the workshop in which we would be undergoing a shedding of the old, as a snake sheds its skin, to be reborn in new form.

Our adventure would take place in Kiakim, an octagonal building nestled deep in the forest. A winding trail through the old-growth forest led to the heavy oak door. That night we entered quietly, respectfully, to find that the interior had been set up with altars in each of the four directions. Against a backdrop of bright cloth, Richard and Donna had placed shells, dolls, carvings, pictures, crystals and other beautiful and significant objects. Their intention was to create a sacred and nurturing space in which we could experience our shamanic death and rebirth.

The first evening we introduced ourselves and spoke about our intentions, our hopes and fears for this workshop, our longings. Many people were full of pain and grief over broken relationships, betrayals or material loss. Only a few had studied the shamanic way or the teachings of this path.

We gathered on the verandah of the main lodge each morning in the sun until the call came from the Tibetan bells played by Richard and Donna as they led us into Kiakim. It was like a celebration of our journey from ordinary reality into sacred shamanic space.

The weather, the sun and rain, the moonlight on the ocean became my touchstone with the "real world" during that week as I moved into a deeper, non-ordinary reality. I remember a feeling of being separate from the participants attending other workshops, that they were living in some world I was no longer part of. The disconnection from ordinary reality began on the first day and built until the initiation.

The first three days were spent in preparation; leaving the reality of day-to-day life behind through a variety of visualizations and writing exercises, and opening our senses so that we could fully experience the drama that was about to unfold during our initiations. We had been examining our lives and the things that would hold us to this earthly plane. We each pondered questions: What holds you here? What beliefs, what objects? On

90

your deathbed what will you miss the most? This is what to let go of. One man's Corvette held him here, another man's children held him. My family and the beauty of the Earth held me captive.

Lines from a TV show called "Babylon 5" kept echoing through my mind: "Lay down the burden of life, surrender yourself to death. Become what you can be when you are no longer afraid, when you know who you are, and why you are, and what you want. When you are no longer looking for reasons to live, but can simply be. Surrender to death, the death of flesh, the death of fear, step into the abyss and let go."[4]

Through meditations, guided imagery and questions to consider at our special places in nature, we were led slowly to the abyss. Twenty-four hours of fasting and meditation would culminate the next morning with our emergence into the dawn. The call came at nine o'clock in the morning, and a subdued and hesitant group wound its way up the path, through the forest to Kiakim. The day was spent in meditation and contemplation of all that might hold us here and of probing deep into our being to find if we were truly willing to let go, to surrender all things, to be in need of no thing from this day on.

Serious stuff, I thought, not something to be played with. All of a sudden I felt like a little child trying to be an adult and not really understanding. Was I ready? Could I really let go of this completely and why would I want to? Somehow my spirit kept calling me forward into a new future, into the unknown. I wondered what awaited us there.

The drum called us again through the inky blackness at midnight to begin our journey into madness, into the abyss of death and, ultimately, into the dawn of rebirth. As we quietly entered the sacred room, we were a group filled with anticipation and courage, prepared to meet whatever the night had in store for each one of us. We made ourselves comfortable on the floor with pillows and blankets. This experience would last until dawn and probably far beyond.

For the next 45 minutes slides were projected on the wall and ceiling. Pictures of the Earth and human behavior, of the horrors and atrocities of war, of violence to the elderly and the children, of sado-masochistic acts, and of the beauty and serenity of sunsets and mountains, the magnitude of the ocean, of friendship and acts of loving kindness were flashed every few seconds.

As I watched I saw two pictures side by side. One was a black-and-white slide of a young Vietnamese man in his mid-teens walking along a jungle road. He had a severed head in each hand. He held the heads by the hair, blood coagulated around their throats. I will never forget his face; it had the look of someone out for a stroll, bringing home items of honor. It was a gruesome scene and yet the honest spirit of a human being shone through his face, with his commitment to his beliefs and values.

Beside this picture was a colored one of my 15-year-old son in his private-school uniform. The juxtaposition was striking. As my father often remarked "There but for the grace of God go I." I knew in that moment that I could not judge these boys as good or bad, right or wrong.

The place, time and culture of birth defined the road each of these young men would travel. And who was to say who had the most difficult journey? In the eyes of the world the judgment would be clear and yet as I pondered those two pictures I knew the beauty of each of their spirits, shaped by circumstances and belief, by doing what they had been taught was right. I knew that as much as I was reflected in the face of my son, so I was reflected in the face of that young man from Vietnam.

I could not hold a position of love for one and hate for the other at the same moment. All that I could experience looking at them was an overwhelming sense of forgiveness and release for them both. They each had their road to walk, as I had mine, and justice and retribution would be a part of those roads as it is for all of us, if not in this lifetime, then in the next.

In that moment, it was incomprehensible to me to choose between those two; to love one and hate the other; one foreign, one familiar; one enemy, one friend. I caught a glimpse of a vision greater than the duality of those two slides. I was experiencing the interconnection of all life and the unity of our spirit. The abyss drew closer as I let go of separation, of division and of illusion.

As I lay on the mat in Kiakim my perceptions began to drift freely in the chaos that had been created by the pictures. My brain had so many contradictory images to try and hold simultaneously that it was pushed to the brink of reason and orderly, logical thought. My mind was trying to understand itself and the world it had created. It could not hold onto rigid beliefs much longer.

The slide show was a complete picture of the paradox and mystery of our world, the horror and atrocities, the beauty and compassion. These were the things that the heart understands and the mind struggles with.

The soft drumming began building in the darkness, reaching a crescendo that signaled the beginning of our shamanic journeys, this night of our "death." I began to lose any sense of time as I slipped further into the rhythm of the drums, riding their heartbeat into the next realm, the three worlds of the shaman. Slowly, below the beat of the drum I began to hear the sobbing and crying of people screaming in their pain. It was a large room and the sound echoed from the walls, confusing even my sense of sound in that space. In time there remained only the voice of pain screaming and the heart of the drum beating.

I began to see an old black-and-white movie of an insane asylum. With the thought that I was taking part in an old movie scene, laughter emerged from my belly. Rolling around on my mat I laughed at the madness of our world and the insanity of our tight hold on our realities. I laughed the laugh of the insane, and experienced profound release; I finally embraced insanity for an instant, and let go of the fear of being crazy which had held me captive for so long. From then on, the label of crazy had no power. As my laughter mixed with the screaming and pain around me I entered into bedlam and true chaos, where thought had no meaning because there were no longer any fixed reference points in reality. This was a world of darkness, the Lower World of the three worlds into which the shaman journeys.

Deeper and deeper the rhythmic heartbeat carried me until I sensed that I was at the edge of a river in almost complete darkness. The river bank beneath my feet was slippery with muck; no edges for even a plant to grab hold of. It emerged from a black void and flowed in front of me. I looked at my feet and I could sense a raft bumping against the shore. The rhythm of the water, the raft and the drum joined together as I slowly raised my gaze to look across the oily black waters. My heart was pounding along with the drum as I saw a figure shrouded in black robes on the far shore, its hand beckoning to me.

Tentatively, I stepped onto the raft, having nowhere else to go. Some unseen force drew it slowly across the river. I expected the "monster from the deep" to leap out of the depths and upend the raft, tossing me into the blackness, lost forever in madness. This is one of the dangers of the Lower World and the blackness of our unconscious that it represents.

Reaching the other side, I stepped off onto the slimy shore with the help of the raftkeeper. Behind him was a rock cavern filled with glowing crystal skulls. They sat on ledges carved out of the rock and gave an eerie quality to the scene as the raft-keeper gestured to me to ascend a flight of stone stairs cut into the side of the rock face leading above the grotto. Climbing up those damp stones I reached the top of the staircase and looked back over the grotto and river. I could dimly see other people slowly drifting across the river. It was deathly quiet.

A sea of swirling, dazzling liquid stretched as far as I could see. My feet were on a solid, black surface that lay behind me to the stairs down to the river and there were only brilliant fiery hues in front of me. The liquid gradually formed into a flat spiral swirling around a central plume of light. Could I step off my solid footing? How much faith did I really have? The swirling spiral appeared solid and with one step I was spiraling toward the vortex at the center. As I reached the plume and entered into it I was transported into one of the stone heads on Easter Island.

"Finally," I thought, "the Middle World!"

Standing there, I knew I had successfully completed the journey into the Middle World, the world that is most like the one in which we live, and is most familiar.

I felt the stone breathing with the life of its creators and my breath began to resonate in harmony. An ancient crone dressed in South American attire appeared and drew me out of the stone. She gestured for me to accompany her. We traveled together for what seemed like days over an uneven path through the grass. After giving me a strangely shaped drum, she led me to a group of ancient ones sitting in the circle of community. I looked into the eyes of the elder sitting in the north. His dark green eyes mesmerized me and I stood entranced. He said my learning had just begun.

I realized that my journey to the Upper World, the high place of Spirit, would have to wait for another time. This descent into madness and psychic death had taken six hours and the drum was calling us home.

As I raised my foot to step across the threshold of Kiakim into the pale light of the summer dawn, dew glinting on the edges of leaves with rainbow light from the reborn sun, my experience of our physical reality was intense and vibrant. Ideas, images, new thought connections were pouring into my mind, into my consciousness as I moved out into a new world.

In a flash of insight, I realized that the journey had resulted in the conscious realization of a new dimension of myself. The release of my fear of being crazy had opened a new universe with a new way of being, one of psychic proportions.

CHAPTER SIX

THE WAY OF THE PSYCHIC

PSYCHIC READINGS

IT SEEMED LIKE a very long and difficult road that had led me, on that January morning, to answer the ad for psychics in the newspaper and make the phone call to Florida. It had lasted almost half a century but I was finally willing to make being psychic a conscious part of my life.

During the first week, the pattern of my days began to settle into a predictable routine. Each day I was out and about, a fairly typical housewife, tending to the activities and chores that keep a house and family running smoothly: buying new runners for my son, toothpaste for my husband, and perhaps a treat for dessert. Then, after dinner as the others settled down in front of the TV to watch the news and see what had happened in the world and in the lives of people across the country, I would take my cup of tea and retreat into my office.

Surrounding myself with golden light and an envelope of blue light, as I had learned during my shamanic training on Cortes

Island and also in the consciousness workshop on Gabriola Island, enabled me to be completely open and aware, letting negative energies pass by. Candlelight flickered off the crystal ball held by my statue of Merlin, a wise wizard keeping watch beside my phone.

This set the stage for my adventure into the world of remote sensing and reading pictures from people's lives all over North America, since the Psychic Line was an international network. Countless miles of phone line and microwave relay stations connected people from their homes to the switchboard in Florida and then to my phone in Victoria, bringing their voices and the pictures and stories of their lives into my office — and my psyche.

My sense of anticipation was heightened that first night. What would this be like? At least the phone line was anonymous; no one who phoned would know who I was or would be able to find me if I made a mistake. I drew comfort from that anonymity, and used it to quell my fears of disaster.

And then the phone rang. I almost leaped out of my skin! "Who's nervous?" I laughed at myself.

My evenings took on the quality of a dramatic mystery, unfolding to flickering candlelight, punctuated by the shrill ring of the phone.

I answered with the prescribed introduction: "Hello, you've reached Dyan at extension 4954. Make sure you note the extension number so that you can call back if you want to."

I never knew what the caller would say. "Are you really a psychic?" could be the first challenging question from someone more interested in disproving me than in listening to the information I was receiving.

Sometimes it was, "All I want to know is my lucky 649 lottery number." The only problem with that was, I have trouble with numbers. If I could find winning numbers, I'd be on a beach in the Caribbean sipping a Margarita.

What I didn't realize that first night was that the calls would range from hilarious to deadly serious. The calls could only be eight minutes long, due to government regulations, and I wanted to move quickly into the reading so that it was as complete as possible in such a short time.

Closing my eyes, I would get a sense of what was happening for the caller, the intense feelings related to their lives. In that sensing there was an element of interpretation: "What would this feeling indicate for me?"

As I relaxed, and accepted the implausibility of this line of work, of telling people about their lives and futures from 3,000 miles away, the feelings came more quickly and completely. Then the pictures started. I was transported into another person's life, their story, their reality.

Awestruck. Astonished. These words rebounded in my head after each call, after each reply of "How did you know that?" or "Wow, you're absolutely right."

Usually the first picture would relate to the caller's most pressing issue, often regarding relationships and finance. Many people were seeking hope and reassurance that they were on the right path, that their lives would work out okay. Some had specific questions about the faithfulness of their partners or the future of their children; some wanted specific details, like the man in Winnipeg who wanted to know exactly what his business competition was up to.

Each evening I would meet a host of down-to-earth people who were seeking answers and encouragement, and my heart was touched by their struggle to live good lives and find happiness.

And then there were people who were confused and in turmoil about their lives. They wanted information about a way through the chaos of their day-to-day worlds, information which might aid them in making a more informed choice, like the woman in Halifax who was drawn to return to school at mid-life and wondered if the cost would be worth it, and the man in Toronto who wanted to know if now was the time to sell his condominium. And always the age-old questions of the heart, about who they were going to marry or if their current lover would marry them.

The hardest calls were the ones from people in deep pain and anguish, people who had lost a partner or a child or who were seriously ill or dying. One woman started the call by saying, "Tell me about the rest of my life." The word "rest" gave the phrase a peculiar, fatalistic ring. As I closed my eyes and looked at her energy, I could see that she was dying from lung cancer and would probably be dead by summer if she kept on this particular path.

"It looks like you have a bad cough. Perhaps you should get it checked out by your doctor," I suggested.

"I do have a bad cough and it's been getting worse. Do you think it would help if I quit smoking?" came the response, and then, "I haven't been to the doctor for a long time. Do you think it's important?"

My heart went out to her, knowing what I knew. "Yes," I replied softly, "it's important." And then we moved on to other areas of her life.

As I worked on the phone line my awareness began to build but I had many questions about my readings and what was happening. Until I found some answers, I followed the directions I received intuitively, trusting that the messages would be for the highest good of my clients on the other end of the phone.

It seemed similar to dream interpretation. The psychic pictures were often metaphorical, analogies of the person's life filled with signs and symbols. I imagined that my client was sitting in the middle of a movie theater, with their spirit as the projectionist; I was merely the screen, reflecting back to them what their spirit wanted them to pay attention to.

Going in blind, I seldom knew what pictures I would see when I closed my eyes and when the energy of the reading was flowing; the pictures would become a rapid slide show of the client's past and future. This kind of reading is like tuning a radio. Everyone and everything is "broadcasting" all about themselves on many different levels or "frequencies."

Palms, the iris of the eye, musculature and meridians, and the etheric or energetic bodies can all be read, to name a few. Perhaps there's a health channel, an emotional channel, a relationship channel, a spiritual channel for each of us. Often we accidentally tune in, and call it a "hunch" or intuition. Practice

99

will increase our ability to tune in to any number of frequencies with accuracy.

When I was on the phone, in those first few weeks, I learned that thinking about what my client was saying in a logical, rational manner, analyzing it, and in fact trying to find an answer to help or fix the problem would stop the reading and the flow of information. Allowing the mystery to unfold, accepting the pictures, the sounds, the information, provided the keys that the person was seeking, the answers to their questions.

I had to learn to trust in the mystery, in the information, no matter how weird, and I found that willingness to follow the guidance deepens psychic awareness further and can bring us into psychic wholeness.

Statistics courses I had taken at university indicated that the future is based on probabilities. There are trends in collective human behavior, in cultural behavior, and in our individual behaviors and circumstances that indicate the most likely direction and possible future; however, there is always the wild card, the unexpected, the synchronicities.

Of the many possible futures for each of us, each decision we make can move us and contribute to the creation of one particular future; however, a single decision can also entirely shift the outcome, the long-range view.

Tempted to turn away from the psychic world again and hide in the safe, predictable scientific world, I decided to confront my fears and continue working on the phone line. I prayed that the information I received would be for the highest good of all the people involved. I felt awed and humbled when I received psychic information that was accurate and confirmed by my client. I was still the greatest skeptic about this profound mystery.

I thought that Lisa, the only other professional psychic I knew, could be a mentor for me. Maybe she could explain some of this. I wanted to talk to her about all my questions and get some direction about the best way to handle some of these issues. I had gone to Lisa twice to have my palm read. Her readings were factual, practical and accurate; I trusted her integrity. She had been reading palms for 20 years and had encountered almost every circumstance, question and type of person in that time. Even though she didn't receive pictures, she was highly intuitive and could read an amazing amount of information from a client's palm. Lisa and her partner Joan had a company called the Psychic Ring that traveled to do psychic fairs in local shopping malls.

I called Lisa the next week and talked to her. She was able to give me some guidance on how to handle the verbal challenges that I was facing from some of the callers, and how to continue reading despite their comments. She also calmed my fears about working as a psychic.

Lisa called me a few weeks later to ask if I would be interested in doing a fair with them. Three of her regular readers were ill, something that was extremely unusual, and she was desperate for someone to come up to Nanaimo the next day to work with the Ring. What an opportunity — to face my fears and let go of my reluctance — and I panicked.

Again I sat at my kitchen table for a long while, gazing out at the city lights below, trying to choose. Working on the Line was one thing; it was anonymous and safe. No one knew who I was or could find out my phone number or address. This, however, was about sitting in the middle of a shopping mall, for the entire world to see, as a psychic reader.

It was clear that the prospect terrified me and I sat there attempting to figure out what I was afraid of. Nanaimo was only two hours away by car, an easy drive. Lisa had a hotel room booked that I could share with another reader from Vancouver. The arrangements were made; all I had to do was show up. It couldn't have been easier.

This fear that had my palms sweating and my knees trembling made no sense. I had the strong feeling that I would be killed if I did readings in public. I had visions of someone coming up behind me as I was reading and stabbing me with a knife. As soon as I saw that picture I heard an unfamiliar voice in my head, a loud, cruel voice that yelled, "End this heresy, this false seeing into the future which is only God's right to see!!"

101

Well, there, I had it, the source of my fear! I could literally hear those words ringing like a death sentence in my head. The power of that voice took me back in time to the witch burnings, to the persecution of healers as heretics. I had been called a heretic before in my life and I wondered briefly if I had been persecuted as a heretic in some past life. Certainly the intensity of my terror seemed completely out of proportion in this age. Could I walk through this fear now?

Thoughts of the twentieth century and police protection calmed my heart, although my hands were still shaking on the wheel of my car the next day, as I pulled into the mall in Nanaimo. I took my briefcase, looking every bit the business-woman, and with still shaking knees walked up to the front table.

For five days, I was astounded that each time I closed my eyes I began to see pictures of my clients' lives, or their homes, or their families. Drawing on all that I had learned about communi-cation throughout my life, and what courage I could find, I closed my eyes, asked for guidance and vision and, like a radio receiver, tuned in to their particular vibratory patterns. The good news was that I had also learned, finally, to turn the receiver off so that I wasn't always reading. Part of the problem in the past had been that I couldn't control when and from whom I received information. This was a welcome skill that allowed me some privacy and quiet time.

One of the readers, named Anna, was a small, dark woman who barely came up to my chin. She had been in the Arctic at the same time as I had. Although we had both lived and worked in Yellowknife, we had never met; we had to move to southern Vancouver Island before our paths crossed. People had told me for many months that there was a woman who lived up island that I needed to meet. Anna and I had much to share, and it was serendipity that this psychic fair finally brought our paths together through the completely unexpected invitation from Lisa.

One reading I remember from this time was for an older woman, who looked very much like a mother. She sat down at my table and asked what I could tell her about her life. The first picture was of four children, three standing and the fourth lying down, somehow under the feet of the other three. I thought this might indicate that three of the kids were "tormenting" their younger brother as kids sometimes do; however, I just described what I saw.

As I was talking about the picture, I began hearing an anguished male voice saying over and over, "I'm sorry, it was an accident. I didn't see it, I'm so sorry. It was an accident, a foolish accident, it was an accident. I didn't see it. Oh God, I'm so sorry!"

Opening my eyes, I looked at the ashen-faced woman across the little table, with tears streaming down her face. As our eyes met and I handed her a Kleenex, she broke down completely.

When she'd regained her composure enough to speak, she said, "My youngest son was killed in a single vehicle accident late at night and I've tormented myself for years with the thought that it might have been suicide. Thank you so much, for finally setting my heart at rest."

Without question, I had learned that day that life continues after death: that young man spoke through my lips to give his mother the gift of peace.

A middle-aged gentleman sat down at my table one evening and asked for insight into his life. The first picture I could see was of a kayak in a fairly fast-moving stream. He was sitting in the kayak. The unusual thing was that he was there without a paddle. As I described the picture, the kayak floated away into the distance with no maneuverability or chance to change direction.

All I could say, besides describing the picture, was that he needed to do something active to grab hold of his life. (Often the readings are part counseling sessions.) He came back at the end of the week to share some of the decisions he had made, decisions that put him back in charge of his life; put him at the helm, so to speak.

At five o'clock on the last day we dismantled the tables and the blue braided rope that formed the circle within which we worked. We loaded everything into Lisa's van, got into our own

cars and formed a caravan down the highway. I was struck by
how much this resembled the gypsy caravans of old that would
appear in town for a few days and then disappear as quietly as
they had arrived.

Driving home I felt triumphant. I had faced, if not
vanquished, my fears and developed some trust in my abilities as
a psychic reader. The other readers were extremely helpful and
very supportive. Lisa had asked me to continue working with
them at other fairs and I had said yes.

I did several much larger fairs, and a few experiences stand out
in my mind. During the first fair I got accustomed to closing my
eyes, describing the pictures I saw, then opening my eyes to find
my clients in tears.

"How can you know all this?" they would say. "You're
describing my life. Oh my God, how can you see this? You're
absolutely right."

I learned to keep a box of Kleenex handy, and I was continu-
ally astonished. I had the same questions! How could I know
this? The mystery was more than I could comprehend.

To clear my energy body after a reading, I got into the habit
of washing my hands after each client. After a particularly
intense reading, I would sit outside for a while to get back in
touch with the earth. I was thankful for my training at the
workshop on Gabriola on how to see what was beyond my usual
frame of reference and also, more importantly, how to get back
into my body.

I remember one client, a very handsome, middle-aged man,
who sat down across from me for a half-hour reading. As I closed
my eyes I could see a tranquil forest scene with a canoe on a
lake. He was paddling the canoe and singing. There was bright
sunlight reflecting off the water. As I began to describe this scene
another picture started to form underneath it. This was unusual.
The second scene was dark and I could see this man sitting at a
desk with his head in his hands, the picture of despair.

Now I was watching two scenes, both fully developed and
happening simultaneously. I finished describing the first and
then started on the second. Eventually, I asked him if he was on

any medication. Yes, he replied, for manic-depression. That explained the split image.

Later in the week, a younger lady sat down at my table. "I've never been to a psychic before," she said nervously. People seem to think being psychic is something special, rather than a skill that we can all develop.

As I closed my eyes I could see her kneeling under her kitchen sink and I could hear a man saying, "Hurry up, bring me a coffee, come on, hurry up, bring me the paper, hurry up. When's dinner?"

After I described what I had seen and heard, she was in tears. "That's my husband," she said helplessly.

"You seemed to be searching for something you had lost, perhaps a ring, but you likely wouldn't find it under the kitchen sink," I continued.

"You're right. It's my lost love. I feel so empty, so in despair. He never lets up."

We sat for a moment quietly, and then the scene changed.

I could see her pick up a lemon meringue pie from the counter and walk into the living room. Now what, I wondered. She hurled it at her husband who was sitting calmly in the chair watching TV. Then she turned around and stormed out the back door into the garden.

"That's exactly what I do," she said. "I reach my limit, go into the living room and shout some angry words, and then retreat to our back yard."

We spent some time that day talking about the symbol of the pie, about the possibility of picking up the pie, cutting two slices and offering him one instead. She phoned me a couple of weeks later to tell me that life was better, now that she had the idea of sharing the pie instead of throwing it.

A very attractive woman named Olive had an unusual reading in that I saw her moving back east. She said she had no plans to do that. I also saw her with a man who had difficulty walking and who was in pain much of the time. As the pictures developed I could see her sitting on a fence, the man on one side and a building on the other. None of this made any sense to her, or to me, at the time.

105

Olive phoned me a year or so later, from Toronto. She had just listened to the tape of her reading and wanted to tell me what had happened. She had decided a few months after the reading to go back to school in Toronto and had met a man who had back problems. He wanted her to quit her courses and move to northern Ontario to be with him. She couldn't decide, and phoned to ask for another reading.

Another man stands out in my memory. As he sat down I could sense a large presence around him. I closed my eyes and could see a very commanding image of a Native in ceremonial dress. The image began to outline a list of things that this man was to collect and what to do with them. He was supposed to begin his work as a traditional healer.

The man looked at me in amazement. "You just described my great-grandfather, a chief from the Queen Charlotte Islands. I guess I'd better do what he says, or else! I knew he'd been trying to contact me but I didn't want to listen."

I smiled, thinking about my own reluctance.

The more I did this work, the more wondrous the mystery became. I had no explanation for these experiences, at least not one that satisfied my scientific mind. It seemed that as long as I trusted in the experience and was unafraid, information would come to my awareness that helped and benefited my clients. It was like being a channel for some otherworld source, and I realized that there was a greater power functioning here.

TECHNOLOGICAL TELEPATHY

The idea that we exist in a "relational" world, one that is composed entirely of our relationship to each and every thing in our life — living beings, objects, situations — was not new to me. However, I had little appreciation of the depth and breadth of the interconnection. I was to learn that this was a world where there are no accidents, only synchronicity. New meaning was finally brought to the scope of my days through an appreciation of the dynamic nature of this system.

"Hi Trin."

"Well, hello there, Marshhawk," drawled Trinity

The text paraded in a line across the screen of my computer. No context, just the printed word through a microchip and yet I could feel the friendly energy of Trinity's hello.

Lambda Moo was a computer game that I liked to play with my son Devin. We would boot up our computers and meet on the game. It seemed a more likely place to find my computer-oriented teenaged son than around the dinner table at home.

Devin had introduced me to this fantasy game, along the lines of Dungeons and Dragons. It was a developing community, a new kind of society, a cyberspace world, where hundreds of people joined together from all around the world. The concept of an active and growing human community stored on a computer hard drive fascinated me. Between 200 and 250 people were logged on at any one time, each with their own character designed especially for this world.

As a player you can go on quests, fight monsters, increase in skill level, or sit in the living room or hot tub and chat with other people who are sitting around. You can run for government and vote as a citizen on issues of community importance.

This community had an established government, rules of conduct and a social order. It had a geography in cyberspace that included mountains, deserts, seashores and other planets. It had a spaceport, a beach, a castle and all the places that make up the geography of any landscape that is inhabited by people, plants and animals. The only difference is that this one existed in a microchip in an IBM computer in Palo Alto, California. A whole land the size of a postage stamp; a Lilliputian reality made up of bits and bytes.

A society is the outcome of weaving together all the components that make up the collective, and thus true global societies are being born on the Internet. There was a spirit of place there, in the same way that there is in this physical world.

Each of the characters felt different. Even though they were text characters, the energy of the player came through in the printed word, like the wind moving through the leaves of a tree. I realized

107

that the spaces between each word held the energy of the thoughts of the player. Serious, playful, cheeky, somber — the sense of the player was there as well as their character's description.

The character I built was named Marshhawk, a spellsinger and wizard using magic to win her battles, singing spells of immobility or death. In my role as Marshhawk I could command lightning to appear for my defense or cause storms to abate. I'd created a cyber-cottage called Harriers Marsh, with deer, a cat named Blue, and a cozy fire in the fireplace.

There was even a pizza parlor. Trinity and I would go back to Harriers Marsh after wrestling with some dragons or finding a magic spell and order a cyber-pizza to share. We often talked of our days, our hopes and dreams in the real world. Yet we hadn't shared our real world identity, our names, our jobs, or any other details of our lives.

These meetings with Trinity accentuated the distance and cold silence that had grown between Malcolm and me. Where we once used to be quite close, now we were lucky to share stilted conversation at the dinner table. The highlights of my days were questing on the game with Devin, and sharing a fireside chat with Trin.

Then one evening, the safety of this make-believe world was shattered.

"Hey, Trin, how about sharing our real-world names and the like? I'm going off on a trip and I'd like to know who you actually are before I go," I typed.

"Sure, Marshhawk, no problem. My name is Malcolm, I'm six feet tall, 180 pounds, have black hair and a beard, and wear glasses. I live in South Dakota and work as an accountant in my parents' store. How about exchanging phone numbers?"

A feather could have knocked me off my chair as that paragraph built across the screen. Just little letters but they spelt a profound message. These last couple of months I had been questing and sharing pizza with a person who exactly matched the description of my husband, my husband who was asleep in the next room, my husband who was in the process of leaving our marriage.

108

Coincidence or not? This was too improbable even for me.

It's strange how we encounter similar things in our lives, over and over, until we're prepared to change and learn to do it differently. Situations, events, people — we just keep attracting the same thing.

I shut off my computer and went to bed, to think about this another day. I wondered as I lay there that night: what if we hadn't developed computers and the Internet? Would we have developed true telepathy and a direct global connection among all things?

I played the game a few more times and then said goodbye to Trinity so that I could focus on my life with Malcolm, the Malcolm who was there beside me.

FIREWALK

Throughout my life I have kept running into walls, the walls of limiting beliefs, of assumptions, mistaken or otherwise, of false perceptions and illusions. For months I had been asking Spirit to guide me to an opportunity that would teach me about the things that so limit our view of reality.

Malcolm and I came to the mainland from Vancouver Island one chilly winter day to take part in a firewalk. The Strait of Georgia was rolling with swells, the cloudy sky obscuring the sun. During the ferry crossing each of us was wondering about the adventure that would take place that night. My head was filled with thoughts of what lay ahead, the fear that fire provoked and the doubts about my ability to maintain the focus required to cross 12 feet of red-hot coals barefoot. I spent the time confronting those fears and visualizing a successful walk. Driving from the ferry terminal to the freeway, we were lost in thought and meditation in preparation for this event; we had been planning for it over the last six months.

After stopping at a local diner for a light dinner we drove on to the farm and met Julie, the woman who was going to lead the firewalk. The fields stretched out for acres across the level land of the delta south of Vancouver. It was twilight and mist was building.

Thirty people. Thirty brave souls seeking to encounter their ability to control the physical manifestation of their bodies, to focus so completely that they could walk on fire unharmed.

We built a tall, beehive-shaped stack of wood, lit the fire and watched the wood catch in the gentle breeze. The fire was tended by Julie's helper while we went inside and shared our concerns. Fear was evident that night in many of our faces. Could we do it? Could I do it? We shared our fears of getting burned, of losing our focus halfway across the pit, of being unable to start. We talked for three hours before we came out, initiates, to surround the fire.

I believed everyone would be able to do this but me. I was going to challenge that belief head on. We stood in a circle around the fire pit, full of glowing, sparkling embers at 1,200C. This heat sears flesh on contact: so I believed, so I thought I knew. And here I was, about to explore the truth of something I had believed all my life, standing there in bare feet in the pasture grass, my jeans rolled up around my knees.

Julie had spoken with us about fear, about change, about letting go. These were all ideas I knew to be important for growth and evolution, all things I had heard for years. Except now, with this 12 feet of scorching coals stretching in front of me, all the comforting affirmations flew out of the window of my mind and I was left with the stark reality of my belief that fire burns flesh instantaneously.

The heat danced over the surface of the coals, a myriad of twisting gossamer ribbons of transparent tangerine. I was fascinated by the sinuous flowing energy, almost alive, primitive and prehistoric in its sensuous essence.

Fire of creation, fire of destruction, fire of safety, fire of challenge. Many thoughts raced through my mind as I began to develop a sense of the power of this element, the transformation of wood to charcoal, the awesome release of the sun's energy stored over centuries in the tree.

The right time had arrived. I moved to the edge of the pit and stood there confronting one of my deepest fears, the fear of fire and burning. Had I ever been a witch, I wondered, back then in the burning times? I began to focus inside myself; to hold the new belief that these coals would leave my feet untouched. I calmed the fear quaking in my belly, fear being the enemy of concentration, and took a very deep breath.

Standing two steps back from the edge meant I'd have momentum as I reached the first step onto the coals. Slowly, ever so slowly I walked across that red-hot bed. Four times I traversed that gateway between beliefs. All of us walked safely that night, all of us with an experience of stepping outside the limits of this reality.

"Popcorn! It felt like dry, crunchy popcorn," I told my son Devin later, "and my knees got really hot as I was standing in the middle of the fire pit. Some people stood and picked up the coals, letting the red-hot embers fall through their fingers." Disbelief shone brightly on his face.

Yet he jumped at the opportunity to walk on fire on the night of his high-school graduation two years later. He walked across the stage that morning to receive his diploma, a successful end to his high-school career, and he walked successfully that night across the fire into his adult life.

Again that night, as I had so many other times in my life, I wondered what is the nature of our reality? The "true and accurate" beliefs that shape our world? What is illusion, what is truth? How do I discern? I was even more curious, and wanted to find the answers to these questions, or at least gain some comprehension of what was really going on.

CHAPTER SEVEN

SACRED STONES

BETH HILL

THIS WAS JUST like psychometry, I realized, standing in front of a petroglyph at Fulford Harbour on Saltspring Island; it was just like doing a reading using Grandmother's necklace to get a sense of what Grandmother was like. I had come here with Beth Hill, an anthropologist, to visit the site and see if I could get any sense of the creator of this Native rock carving.

The mythical and mystical petroglyphs of the Northwest Coast and other areas of the world have fascinated archaeologists and anthropologists for decades. These enigmatic depictions of human or animal-like beings, of symbols and designs, carved into rock, occur along the coast from Alaska to Washington, and have been made for thousands of years. Many are located along rivers or ocean edges; some are found in remote inland sites of great power.

Petroglyphs comprise a vast range of characters and motifs. A few representations are exact, like the depiction of the paddlewheeler *Beaver* or the sailing vessels at Clo-oose, while others hold intense mystery as to their form and function. Some are clearly discernible as fish or other animals. Many represent human beings, their faces, bodies and especially their eyes. Others are less obvious.

Beth was a wonderful, energetic woman who had studied at Cambridge University and was an expert on Northwest Coast Native rock art. Since petroglyphs cannot be dated and the artists are unknown, she had an intense desire to find out more about the carvers and the time period in which they created the pictures. She turned to psychics and shamans in an attempt to fill in the gaps that science couldn't address.

Our connection was made by a mutual friend, and Beth phoned me one evening to ask if I'd be interested in "reading" some of the carvings for her. I agreed readily, feeling drawn to

Beth Hill.

her voice and the adventure she was offering. The serendipity of my background in anthropology and archaeology did not go unnoticed.

Our first trip was to Saltspring Island to visit two sites that Beth found especially curious and intriguing. She didn't tell me anything about this particular petroglyph before our visit to Fulford. She preferred not to "contaminate" my reading with outside information, and I suspected that she was also seeking psychic validation for what she had already sensed herself. We drove to the park at Fulford, just by the road leading to Ganges. Sitting beside a towering fir, this petroglyph had been carved into the side of a large boulder. The carving was of a stylized face surrounded by a corona. As I stood there gazing at the image, Beth watched intently.

Images began to flood into my awareness, of a time when the face stared seaward into the distance. I had a sense of the waves lapping at the base of the stone, rain clouds building and energy working into cumulo-nimbus shapes as salmon waited to return to the creek. I had a strong sense of the salmon awaiting the rain, the thirst-quenching drops that would enable their return.

One eye of the face seemed to protrude, perhaps looking into the future, the other seeing back into the village with a sense of protection of these shores. The corona encircling the face was reminiscent of the halo that has been used to symbolize a powerful spirit or god in many different cultures.

My trance state slowly ebbed and I walked over to Beth to share all that I had sensed. The villagers had told her that this image was connected with rain, and that it had sat on the shore of the village just down the harbor. I could see the comings and goings of the villagers, their canoes, and their activities. She wanted as much information as I could provide and she verified many of the details in the images.

The main feature that I noticed was the lack of energy in this petroglyph. Usually, objects or features hold the energy of their owner or their creator and the passion of the creative process. Perhaps the energy that had surrounded this carving had been lost when the rock was moved from its original location. It was no longer filled with the thoughts and visions of the villagers. It had become a stone out of place: the connection to its purpose had been severed.

Carrying on with our day, Beth was impatient to get to the next site. We drove around the head of the harbor to look at a bowl-shaped depression carved in a large boulder on the beach. I could see that the bowl had been used for grinding by the markings inside it. I had a sense that many people had used it, one after another, grinding shells, clams, and ochre. I could not sense any ceremony associated with this bowl; it felt eminently practical and useful. It was used to prepare items for ceremony but not used in the ceremony. This bowl had a very strong energetic connection to the petroglyph we had just looked at. We discussed the possibility that some of the substances ground in the bowl were used to paint the petroglyph for ceremonies.

I described this information tentatively at first, thinking that I might be embellishing what I saw with memories from my anthropology courses at university. Beth was open to all information, and when something was different from what she had previously thought, we had great discussions about reasons for the difference: perhaps a different time period, a different cultural group or maybe a different perspective.

We arranged a date for the next month when we would visit the Shamans' Pool in Kulleet Bay near Ladysmith on the east coast of Vancouver Island. I looked forward to the drive up-island with Beth, as we would spend the time talking about everything from her childhood, to teenagers, to spirituality, and of course, psychic phenomena. Our association had begun.

The worldview of the petroglyph carver probably encompassed a cosmology or set of beliefs in which the rocks, forests and oceans were one with the animals, including man, that lived in and on them. This cosmology would posit a unified connection between all things, so that a carving of a salmon would become the spirit responsible for the salmon, and thus the image would be revered or feared as the living spirit itself. Beth suggested during one of our discussions that the petroglyphs express the spiritual attitudes of the coast people, and

115

we enthusiastically debated and explored these ideas during our long drives together.

It was wonderful to enter into these discussions with Beth, for she came from a thoughtful academic and scientific background, while I tended to approach the ideas from a psychic and shamanic point of view.

We started off early in the morning, into the fog and drizzle of a typical autumn day on the west coast. As we drove over the Malahat Beth asked me to tell her something of my past, how I had come to develop these psychic skills and where I had encountered and embraced the practice of shamanism. As I recounted my story, she asked insightful questions and shared experiences from her own life that paralleled mine. She was fascinated by the years I had spent in the Arctic, and the archaeology of that area. She kept asking if I had thought of writing about what I had experienced, if I had thought of telling these stories. I finished the last description just as we turned off the highway, and Beth remarked emphatically, "That's a fascinating story you've told me this morning. That's your book! Start writing."

We drove through the village at Kulleet Bay onto an almost obscured dirt track that led into the trees. Beth mentioned a previous visit she had made with another archaeologist and a psychic; however, she didn't give any of the details.

Beth parked the car, got out and began walking farther into the bush. As I followed her I noticed the edge of an energy field, probably surrounding the site, a tangible "curtain" of energy that, as we walked through it, was like a cloth of soft tingles against my skin.

Even before reaching the pool, I began to sense images. I could see a circle of elders, shamans in their ceremonial capes of painted cedar bark, some short, others long, and painted hats of various designs. They were standing around the pool, although the circle was incomplete, with more people on one side of the pool than the other. As Beth began to clear away the fallen maple leaves, a carpet of gold covering the carved stones and filling the depression of the rock, I could see that the faces carved around the pool exactly matched the circle of elders I had seen.

116

I knelt at one end of the pool and began to open to the spirit of this place, of this sacred site. A rather menacing figure began to form at the opposite end of the pool and grew into a towering form, a spirit of immense proportions, which loomed over us and roared.

This was more than a human image, more than any earthly image I could conceive. Realizing that an offering was needed to show respect to this spirit and the profound history of this site, I asked the spirit to wait a minute as I ran back to the car in search of something appropriate. I found some dates — sacred food in the Middle East. I rushed back to the pool and began my power song, which would call the spirits of the four directions as witness. I laid the dates at the edge of the pool, speaking of our intention that day, to observe this site and honor the spirit of the pool.

Once the protective spirit was appeased, the doorway opened and I was flooded with visions and voices telling one story of the Shamans' Pool. I saw an elder sitting at the edge of the rock where I was kneeling. He sat alone at the beginning, gazing into the pool, seeking guidance. He wore cedar cloth and there were few trees around the pool at that time, the beach being closer to the pool then than it is now. I heard these words to begin the story:

"When we gaze into the pool we are drawn into the sky, flying in brotherhood with the World to find the reasons for our tribe's misfortune, or how we can call the whales back to our beach after the cold. It is our gateway, the opening between these worlds into which we can fly. We dive into the sky from this pool's edge. We are the guardians of the gateway, and we guide and protect the shaman during his flight ... all worlds flow to one."

The picture changed then to show two youths, young men, coming from the sea in initiation, to add their carvings to the growing number of faces around the pool. Perhaps an initiation into the tradition of shamans included bathing in the ice-cold water before adding the eyes to those that had already begun to define the pool's edge. As I watched the youths carving their

117

faces beside the pool on that winter's day so long ago, I heard the spirit speak again:

"We have each come in our own turn, to add our mark to the edge of the pool; to be watchers for our land. We have come alone with spirit to add our face to the circle. In the beginning the World watched as life took form. Each animal and plant was a part of the Spirit of Place ... cedar trees and abalone each had their own role to fill. The World was birthing itself, and would become aware as life became aware. We are to be reminders of the witness. We sit in council watching the World unfold, as our people watch the seasons change. And so we add our eyes to the eyes of the World."

A hush had fallen over the forest glade while the reading was taking place. Beth stood at the side of the pool, gazing at the carvings, her hands at her sides. I walked over to her and as we stood there in the mystical stillness with golden sunlight filtering through the burnished maples, we expressed our gratitude to the spirit of the pool.

On the way back to the car, we paused at the edge of the energy field and had great excitement walking back and forth

The Shamans' Pool at Kulleet Bay. (COURTESY OF RAY HILL)

through the boundary so Beth could get a clear sense of its edge. We sat in the car while Beth taped my reading and I drew the capes and hats that I had seen people wearing. Beth was interested in descriptions of the implements the young men had used, such as fire-hardened wood, hammer stones, pick-like pieces of bone.

Once we finished the business of our trip, we walked over to the beach to eat the lunch we had brought. Sitting in the sunshine on a driftwood log, we shared the magic and mystery of the past hours. Beth described her previous experience at the pool when the psychic who was with her had sensed great danger and instructed everyone to run back to the car and leave the area immediately. We chatted about the possibility that he had sensed the same spirit that I had seen. Obviously there was an energy that protected and defined this sacred power spot. We felt quite blessed at having had the opportunity to witness the power of this site and to be in communion with the spirit that rested there.

On our way home we talked more about spirits and psychic reading, and planned our next outing, a visit to Beth and Ray's home to view a labret that they had found.

Exploring ideas about the purpose and function of petroglyphs, we thought they might depict spirits seen in vision quests, or be representations of anthropomorphic gods, intended to call on the spirits for assistance, or to appease them during times of distress. These depictions would have provided the opportunity to interact directly with the spirit realm, to gain what was needed. In many hunting and fishing cultures, representations of the animals upon which life depended, in the form of amulets or stylized carvings, were used to call the animal to come and offer itself up to feed the group. Done with reverence and sacredness, these carvings were also used to honor the animal's act of giving.

Perhaps by merely showing one person's vision of a spiritually important experience, in some way, the petroglyphs provide a record of man's perception of and interaction with his world. This record from the past, whatever the intention of the carver,

119

brings the energy of that event into the present, and we can wonder at the meaning and mystery.

It was a sunny Sunday, wavetops glinting in Vesuvius Bay, as I sat with Beth and Ray at their home by the ferry dock. Ray reached into a small cloth bag and brought out a labret. It was a piece of stone carved to fit into the lip (usually the bottom lip) of an individual. Labrets are often part of ceremonial dress. I held the small object in my hand and immediately jumped, because my sense of the energy was so strong and so anguished.

I opened to the sensations and began to see pictures of battles, of spears, of axes covered with blood. I could see groups of people striding up an embankment from the ocean, as if going into battle with the people who awaited them at the forest edge. There was a strong sense of death and brutality. It felt as if this had occurred in the distant past and that the battle had been on a rock surface rather than grass or soil. Gradually, I became aware of a young man who wore the labret. He was undertaking purification rituals alone in his shelter, before the battle.

As I completed my descriptions of what I could sense, Beth told the story of finding the labret. Some years later, there was an archaeological investigation and excavation of a site near by, which showed evidence of a battle having occurred during the early history of the area.

We talked of what might have occurred at that site, of wars between tribes, of the tumultuous history of this coast. Planning many more trips, we talked about going up to Marina Island the following summer to look at a series of petroglyphs that appeared to represent whales. They were at the entrance to the channel that led to Desolation Sound and were positioned as if to protect the passage between the islands, or to serve as signs to the migrating whales.

We talked about other ways in which we could explore the energy of the images of the petroglyphs. Beth asked if this kind of reading could be done from a picture and if I would be able to use the book that she and Ray had written documenting the petroglyphs along this coast, *Indian Petroglyphs of the Pacific Northwest*.

I replied that certainly it was possible to use photographs or even a verbal description of the location of the object. We got out their book and sat at the table looking at the drawings. She picked out a couple and asked if I could try to get a story that would tell about the spirit of the carving.

A few days later I sat with one of the pictures that Beth had chosen. I stilled my mind and opened widely to connect with the energy of the petroglyph. As I sat there in the evening beside the fireplace in my living room in Victoria I began to hear distant chanting and faintly I could hear a voice reciting a story. I listened intently and slowly the voice became louder. The story it told was about two brothers on their first hunt and how a petroglyph was created to honor the journey and the new name of the older brother, given to him by the Bear Spirit that he met during his adventure.

When I called Beth the next day she was pleased with the story. While it didn't provide the kind of analytical detail that she often wanted, it did give some insight into the symbolic and mystical nature of the carving. She suggested I work with other photographs and then she mentioned a carved bowl she wanted me to look at on Saltspring Island. We set a date for our journey to Wilson's Bowl.

The day was beautifully sunny when I took the ferry from Sidney to Saltspring Island to meet Beth. The trip across to the island always had a feeling of coming home, because of the summers I had spent there with my parents.

Beth was waiting at the ferry dock with a welcome smile and the glint of adventure in her eyes. Our conversation picked up where it had left off the week before. After driving through Ganges we parked the car and began a lengthy walk along the beach to reach Wilson's Bowl.

This exquisite piece of rock art was carved in a boulder facing seawards. The boulder stood at the edge of the shore and would be covered at high tide. The top had been flattened into a square-shaped surface and the shallow depression was carved with fine craftsmanship. The level of care taken in this carving, and the shapes used, created the impression of a sacred altar, much like the baptismal fonts in our churches.

As I began to sense the energy of this bowl I could see a solitary figure, perhaps a shaman, standing beside it. He had the skeleton of a salmon resting in the bowl, as if to give the bones as an offering back to the sea.

Another picture came, again of a shaman. He was gazing into the still water of this bowl, using the mirrored surface to divine future events and receive information that would answer questions that he had asked of the spirits.

This bowl was close to the location where the labret had been found. Beth was excited to have a description of the clothing of the person using the bowl, and also a confirmation of the purpose of the carving.

As we were standing around the bowl talking about these pictures, I began to get a sense of another picture, although this one was far in the distance, farther away in time. I could see another shaman, holding a salmon high above him so that the inner organs could fall to the ground. He appeared to be using these to discern the future, or perhaps the reason for some catastrophe that had befallen his village. His dress was less finely crafted than in the previous pictures.

While I was happy to be able to see these pictures and provide Beth with a greater sense of what might be going on, sometimes the gaps in the information were frustrating. How did these series of pictures relate to each other? What were the shamans seeking and why? I wanted to know, yet I was unable to gain access to this level of detail.

One day later in the summer Malcolm and I accompanied Beth, Ray and an anthropologist from the mainland to a site on Wallace Island. That Saturday dawned grey and cloudy. Beth called early to say the trip was on despite the weather and that she and Ray would pick us up just after nine o'clock.

Ray drove across Saltspring to Fernwood, where we met Mark, an anthropologist who had worked extensively with Native groups in the northern regions. He thought he might have discovered a shamans' bowl and was hoping that Beth could verify his find. We piled into his Zodiac and crossed the water to the north end of Wallace Island.

Once we landed on the island we hiked to the site on a promontory jutting out into the sea. Beth and Ray examined the bowl, and from the look on Beth's face when she initially saw it, there was no doubt that Mark was going to be disappointed. They felt around the circular depression and scooped out much of the water to examine the bottom and sides. Then Beth asked me to read the energy of the area, especially this cup-shaped hollow.

I could get no sense from the bowl or the area immediately around it. It felt like a natural feature in the rock outcrop. As I sat there trying to see if this feature had any significance as a shamans' bowl I was aware of strong energy behind me, among the trees. I told Beth that it seemed like something that the sea had made. Then I went over to the grove of trees, said a prayer asking for deeper opening, and sat quietly.

The promontory on Wallace Island that Beth and Dyan investigated.

123

I began to get impressions of canoes on either side of the promontory, of a great deal of activity, a waypoint, and a staging area for canoes and travel up and down the channel. No one had lived here, but lots of people had stopped on their way to somewhere else. I described that to Beth and Mark.

I sat while they began lunch and scanned the energy of this area for other pictures. A picture slowly began to form in my mind's eye, one about a burial, a very quiet burial, people bringing a man to be placed on the island. He was on a skin stretcher as they carried his body from their boat.

A young woman stayed alone to burn some intimate things. She placed them in the rock hollow as part of a private ceremony of release for his spirit, and also to ensure that no one could steal his power as a great hunter. After everything was gone she filled the hollow with seawater and gazed into it; the feeling was of great sadness, of wanting to know where he had gone.

I described the clothing and skin boat to Beth and Mark, drawing pictures to augment my verbal report. This type of boat was not usually known along this part of the coast, but was found farther to the south. Perhaps this was a time when the southern peoples lived over more of the coast than they had recently.

It was clear that we needed to collect information from both the physical, scientific field and the metaphysical, symbolic field to gain a more complete picture of what had happened on any site.

On the trip home we talked about the following summer and trips to other sites, especially Marina Island. As always, we talked of many things, yet our conversations were becoming focussed on the idea of a Spirit of Place, the essential spirit of our landscape and each rock, stone, tree or glade within it.

This was the world of ley lines, power spots and sacred groves, a world that fascinated Beth. We encounter it when we experience the energy of old-growth forests as somehow different from the energy of a deserted beach, or an alpine meadow. Beth knew this spirit intimately, having spent each summer for almost 30 years boating through the wilderness of coastal British Columbia and writing about it. We talked about our adventures and the book that was waiting to be written, about this sacred spirit.

But within days all this changed. Our adventures were placed on the shelf as Beth was diagnosed with a recurrence of cancer and told she had only months to live.

I treasured each time with this woman who was mentor, friend, confidante, and mother to me. The thought that there was a limit to our moments together brought great sadness to my heart. Even though I knew that a wonderful world awaited us after death I wanted her here — now. Beth, ever curious, was excited to be on the journey that would take her to the answer to one of the greatest mysteries for mankind — what awaits us after death.

Our travels together had a bittersweet tinge as we realized that our spirit book might never be written and that we would never go to Marina Island together. I spent time with her that winter on Saltspring Island as she was writing her last book, *Moonrakers,* content with whatever precious time she had to spare during this mysterious and sacred journey at the other end of life. Beth completed this part of her journey at home in January 1997. Her picture sits above my computer while I work, and I miss her.

CHAPTER EIGHT

UNSEEN FORCES

INNER SPACE AND SUBTLE ENERGY

MY EXPERIENCES WITH Beth Hill, and her illness, caused me to question the objective and benefit of my psychic ability. What was its purpose? Seeking the answer to this single question opened up new doors in my life. With my willingness to move fully into the psychic realm of subtle energy, finally, I realized I wanted to know more. I wanted to learn how to use this to help people and our planet.

Reading energy with clairvoyant sight is much like reading a book with normal sight or perhaps more like reading the newspaper in which we get only the highlights of a person's life story. The paper can be opened at the beginning, or at any page until the end.

I had come to an understanding that, in terms of the psychic world, there is no concept of time or space; seemingly all things happen simultaneously, so "seeing" becomes merely a matter of where to look.

My encounters with illness and issues of health and healing began to combine with the idea of reading energy as I started to work with one of the doctors in my city on a project that explored the use of intuitive medicine in patient care. Ken had been Beth's doctor so it was little surprise to me when we connected on this project.

Intuitive medicine is the work pioneered by Caroline Myss, Ph.D., and Norm Sheeley, M.D., using psychic sight to look for the energetic origin of the disease present in the patient. This was basically like the health reading I had learned at the workshop on Gabriola Island; however, this went further, into exploration for the cause of the disease. Ken had given me the initials of ten people and asked me to scan their energy to see where and what disease was present. He told me nothing other than their initials. I didn't even know if they were his patients.

I spent one Saturday sitting with the initials, trying to get a sense of what was happening in the body of the patient. One gave the impression that the muscles in his back were in knots and the skeletal structure was misaligned. I wrote down lower back problems. I looked further in the hope of finding the origin and I could see that he was picking people up incorrectly. Symbolically, he was lifting and carrying the weight of many people on his back, people who should have been carrying their own problems, their own weight.

A third set of initials prompted a feeling of longing for a child. I wondered what that might mean and as I scanned the person I could see that her ovarian tubes were blocked with fibrous growth. The likelihood of a child was remote and had prompted a bout of depression.

When I got to the sixth set of initials I heard a despairing voice cry, "Help me, please help me." This voice was very distant and sounded as if it was coming from the middle of a storm or down a long tunnel. The energy field of this person felt extremely chaotic, swirling and spiraling every which way, and was very black. I wrote down that this patient had late-stage cancer and was in great pain. The blackness had a peculiar quality to it. It was more than an absence of light; it was a tangible, absorbing blackness, like a black hole in space. More than diseased tissue, the cancer had the quality of being a living, black substance, as if it had transformed the tissue into a different vibration or stage of growth.

I finally reached Ken two weeks later and gave him the information I had sensed. He confirmed what I had seen although it was clear that I had a lot of work to do learning anatomy. He wanted to know when I had done the readings, and told me that I had scanned the lady with cancer five days after she had died. It was no wonder that the energy of her body was so chaotic.

It gave me a chilling feeling to have heard her voice crying for help in the swirling turbulence of energy after her death. I wondered what I could have done to help her, perhaps to reach out in some way so that she could know that she wasn't completely alone and lost. I tried to reach her again but was unsuccessful. Her energy had dissipated.

The application of psychic second sight had its frustrations. I worked with a lovely woman who was recovering from cancer, another of Ken's patients. She was jubilant that her tests were finally clear of any indication of cancer, and we celebrated this great news.

Then I woke up one morning about eight months later, thinking of her and knowing that the cancer had returned. I relayed that information to Ken who said he had seen her just one week before and there was no sign that the cancer had returned. She seemed completely clear. A year after I had that conversation with Ken, she was diagnosed with a recurrence of the cancer. As Ken told me this, we looked at each other with anguish. Could anything have been done, could treatment have started even though there was no physical evidence that the cancer had returned? Could this have been stopped? We had no answers.

We carried on with the project and discovered that each time, the information and the benefit that it brought were different. I finally learned how to "not see" by switching off the sight, rather than blocking it completely and setting up walls so that I wouldn't be overwhelmed by another person's experience. Now I had a choice.

In line with my shamanic teachings, I would only use this way of seeing if I was asked. Otherwise, it was a serious boundary invasion. It seems that, as a culture, we have very few psychic boundaries and this manner of seeing is very powerful, and very intimate. It made sense ethically to follow the teachings of wiser cultures and allow each person to ask for information when they were ready to receive it.

At this time I was working out of a shop advertising psychic readings in the traditional fashion as well as continuing the project with Ken. I had been prompted by my guides to become more public in offering psychic readings. Since I knew the owners of this delightful New Age store, it seemed like a comfortable and safe place to work.

Charlotte called one evening to ask for a reading. She wanted to know what her future held and if she would find a partner soon. As I was driving to her home I began to get a sense of a dark, towering presence, like a skyscraper bending earthward — black and wide. I could feel it on my right side, leaning over me. I thought this might be an entity that wanted to make its presence known to Charlotte. I began to ground more strongly than I usually did and prepare myself by strengthening my boundaries so that I could channel this being if necessary, and remain unaffected by it. I wondered about the quality of the energy, though. It seemed menacing and very black.

After Charlotte and I were settled I began to open for the reading and got an impression of the black entity. It was massive and shrouded, wearing a large, broad-brimmed hat and a black garment like a shroud. (I should have been getting a clear picture of who this being represented; there were enough clues.)

Its face was completely in shadow but not black. I could make out its form but few details. I had a sense that now was the time for Charlotte to accompany it; the time to do what she already knew had to happen. After I relayed this information to Charlotte, she asked, "Where does he want me to go?" I relayed this question to the shrouded figure and added that she was fearful.

It indicated a large pool of black liquid and extended its arm toward Charlotte, although its hand was still enclosed in its sleeve. As I experienced the fear in the pit of Charlotte's stomach, the entity extended its hand from the sleeve so that she could grasp it. My first impression was that the hand was brilliant white light, glowing as if it was radioactive. As I looked closer I also saw that it was skeletal, only bones, no flesh, and radiant with a strange light that had a slightly greenish tinge in the whiteness, a phosphorescent appearance. It wanted Charlotte to take its hand and walk into the liquid pool to submerge in the chaos of transformation.

Charlotte was dying, as she suspected, but she had been unwilling to admit it. She decided to go to the doctor as a result of this image, and after an operation and chemotherapy for the cancer she began the journey back to health. This reading shook me to my very core. The idea that disease has a personality and presence all its own was quite radical to me, yet this was the persona of her cancer, and also the face of her fear.

Sometimes the information came unbidden. I had gone to a house that was advertised for rent, thinking that it might be the right place for me to move after my house sold. As I walked up the sidewalk toward the front door a lovely Persian cat, meowing stridently, obviously wanting attention, greeted me. I wondered what she was trying to tell me.

At the door I was greeted by a roly-poly cocker spaniel. As I reached down to pat her I had the thought, "Oh poor pup, you have a tumor in your belly." It was that simple. Just a passing thought, quite innocent in its form, merely an observation. The dog's owner said that the dog had been very healthy and showed no indications of disease, so I left it, thinking that I must have imagined it.

The spaniel died two weeks later of a cancerous tumor in its abdomen. It was so easy to discount that still, small voice, to disregard it in favor of the physical evidence, to ignore what my heart knew to be true.

Even our diseases are readily found in our energy fields, a storybook waiting to be opened. Perhaps with conscious awareness, we can choose to re-write the end of the story. Energetically, it appears that all "dis-ease" begins spiritually and

then filters through the emotional levels until it become observable physically. It takes time for this process to happen and we
often get fair warning of what's coming when we finally listen to
the spiritual and emotional whispers.

Ken called me to work with Rita, a patient of his who was
often overcome with panic attacks and debilitating weakness for
no apparent reason. Rita could function fairly well around her
home, but going out to shop or to friends' homes was a major
event, and left her exhausted for days.

I met Rita in her home, a charming townhouse. She had been
to many doctors and counselors in an attempt to uncover the
source of her trauma. We chatted about her experiences and I
began to get flashes of a rough-hewn cabin wall. There was no
such cabin in her present life.

I asked her to close her eyes and become very still. I began to
describe the picture I was seeing and she replied that it was a
place that she had often seen in nightmares. She began to
describe the dreams so that I could "see" them. The story started
to flow and as she described being too afraid to look out the
window, I could tell her what I was seeing through the glass.

There came a point in the story when we both had the sense
of an older woman telling her not to worry. I prompted Rita to
ask this spirit for a gift that she could bring back to the present
to help her dispel the energy of her illness. The woman gave her
a beautiful soft turquoise blanket. I encouraged Rita to gather up
any of her energy that might still be caught in this story and to
cut her ties to the drama and we came out of trance and back to
the present.

Rita sat still for quite a while, holding the blanket psychically
in her lap. The blanket had a tangible presence; she said she
could feel the weight in her lap and the softness on her hands.
As we talked, she remembered her older sister giving her a
blanket for her birthday many years ago. She could also see the
connection between the woman in the journey and her sister.

Now she had a tool to work with. The next day, when she
went out with her husband, instead of sitting in the car she
went into the bank with him. As the panic attack started, she

131

took the blanket energy and wrapped herself with it. The panic stopped immediately.

Rita's life assumed a sense of normalcy it hadn't had for years. After a few months, she no longer needed to use the blanket energy, although she knew she would have it available if necessary. The next time I saw her she was vibrant and alive, free to come and go as she pleased.

It seems that when we find the energetic beginning of the condition, the block that is creating the problem or the disease, things improve and healing takes place. The block is like a festering sore that can begin to improve when it is finally opened to light and air and cleansed of fear. Rita went back to the original wounding, brought it into her awareness and moved through the experience without blocking it by fear. She also received the blanket, a gift from the spirit world to act like a bandage until healing was completed.

ENCOUNTERS

There are subtle energies all around us, "other world" realms that we enter occasionally — sometimes accidentally, sometimes with purpose. Ghosts are often surprise encounters, disembodied spirits come to help or harm. They are usually startling; we catch sight of them out of the corner of our eye or sense them as they move past.

While I was in university I had worked part time for an archaeological consulting firm and had the opportunity to spend the summers out on excavations or conducting surveys of the back-country areas in southern Alberta. Days were spent hiking the logging roads of the area, in solitude, searching for places that might hold archaeological sites and traces of Early Man. The thick mountain forests, however, obscured any remains that may have endured through the last 10,000 years.

Camped on the side of the lake in Crowsnest Pass, deep in the Rocky Mountains, six women on the University of Calgary crew shared a bunkhouse at a tumbled-down resort that we used during our summer field season. One night, as we were drifting off to sleep, a light moved slowly through the back wall and into the bunkhouse. It floated about three feet above the floor, a small, round, yellow globe slowly swinging back and forth. Four of us saw the light and the shadowy form that was holding it. Incredulous eyes watched as it walked through the building and out the front window.

A hush fell over the room, as Kate whispered, "Did you guys see that?"

"What was it?" came the reply. We discussed various alternatives, being good analytical university students, and eventually fell asleep.

The next day we found out the local story about the ghost of the pass, a railway man whose job it was to inspect the tracks at night with his lantern. Crowsnest Pass is an area of many rock falls along the steep cliffs of the mountains, and he looked for new slides that blocked the track. After he was killed, it seemed that his spirit was stuck here, so he kept on walking the tracks in death as he had in life.

A second experience with a departed being the next year clearly confirmed for me the existence of spirits in this physical plane. I spent the summer at my parents' home on Saltspring Island. I was making lunch in the kitchen on one of those deliciously hot summer days by the Pacific Ocean, with the earth smelling sweetly of the full bloom of summer plants. As I reached into the fridge, I heard loud, agonizing breathing from the bedroom. It sounded like someone gasping frantically and groaning in extreme pain. My first thought was for my mother and the possibility of a heart attack. I raced into the bedroom and found it empty. I tore around the house, shouting, "Mom, where are you?" Not finding her, I looked out the back to see my mother digging in the vegetable garden. I walked up the lawn and described my experience to her.

"Oh yes," she said, "that's the woman who used to live here. She died of lung cancer in the bedroom. I imagine her last days were difficult. I hear her sometimes." Mom said it calmly, as if meaning that the woman still lived there too.

Some years before, I had been in a hospital emergency room when a young man died from injuries suffered in a car accident.

133

Suddenly, while I sat there, a hot, thick, vibrating wind that felt and sounded like a blast from a speeding freight train rushed past and through me.

As the wind hit my body I toppled off my seat from the force and the shock. Righting myself, I looked around the emergency room to see everyone continuing matter-of-factly as if nothing had happened. Again, as so many times before, I wondered what had just happened, and why no one else had noticed.

Upon inquiry, although no one else had felt the wind, I learned that it had occurred at the very moment of the young man's death. I could only surmise at the time that it was his spirit that rushed past me in the explosion of his release.

These experiences were beginning to weave together to indicate to me that conventional ideas of death did not account for such contacts, and that perhaps death was only a shift in energy patterns, from the dense physicality of the body to the lightness of the spirit.

The experiences of my childhood introduced me to the angels and guides that kept me company on my Earth walk. Always gentle and encouraging, although somewhat austere, they would guide me in my dreams to new experiences. As time went on, they would leap out at me through books, through chance meetings, through the synchronicity of life when it is "in the flow." Whenever I felt alone, unhappy and without direction, a message would come, an indication of new possibilities unfolding. Even though my guides had been in my dreams for most of my life, I had studiously avoided meeting them in any conscious way.

One winter's day in Yellowknife, while I was perusing the shelves of our local bookstore, a small paperback book called *Channeling: Meet Your Spirit Guides* caught my attention. There it was resting unassumingly on the shelf, sticking out farther than all the other books. How could I resist picking it up?!

That evening, after the boys were safely in bed, I lit a fire, put on some music and settled down for an interesting exploration into the idea of channeling. It was a very quick read and when I reached the "how to" part I decided to try it.

After reading the instructions, I stretched out on the couch and began to empty my mind, as instructed. I visualized becoming an empty vessel, like an empty bottle, so that a spirit or guide had room to enter and flow through me.

Being ever so naive, I thought this could be fun and interesting. I had said a prayer to my guides asking for insight and protection, and for the highest energy possible to come through me. As I lay there, relaxed and open, letting the sounds of the music from the stereo drift through my mind, I heard a deeply masculine voice echo loudly in my head.

"Hi," it seemed to bark. "I'm Peter, your guide. I am a shepherd tending my flock and I have come to be with you for this time."

My instantaneous reaction was to scream, "GET OUT OF MY HEAD!" Having a disembodied male voice that I didn't recognize actually speak to me from inside my head was too much, way too much. I put the book away, not knowing how to handle the experience.

Yet my encounters with spirits that stayed external to me seemed to be acceptable. Over the years, with practice, I learned to relax into deeper encounters. There was sometimes an element of confusion in these encounters with apparently disembodied spirits. In my first few experiences with channeling I would think, "Oh, I'm just making this up." Then, as it continued, I would realize that there was a different voice talking in my head and I would panic.

However, the more I could allow in the experience of these unique energies, seemingly different from myself, the easier it was to discern "who's talking" and "who's thinking," without becoming overwhelmed and frightened. Nevertheless, the label of "crazy" echoed through my mind.

One day at church in Yellowknife I had a physical encounter with yet another form of unique energy. The church I attended held "testimony Sunday" on the first Sunday of each month. At these meetings members of the congregation would stand and give their testimony of how Spirit had worked in their lives and of how they followed Spirit.

On this particular Sunday I felt the prompting to stand and give my testimony. However, I didn't want to. I was tired and cranky and the last thing I wanted to do was stand up in front of all these people and talk. I didn't feel very loving or kind. I had learned that this is exactly the right time to reconnect with Spirit, to come back into alignment, but I can be quite stubborn at wanting it my way.

As I sat there arguing in my mind against standing, I felt a hand rest in the middle of my back for a moment. Then that hand pushed — hard — and I tumbled off the pew. The only way to stop myself from ending up on the floor was to stand. So there I was, standing, with all the members waiting expectantly for me to begin my testimony. I quickly looked behind me to see who could have pushed, and, not surprisingly, the two pews behind us were empty.

I learned that arguing with Spirit doesn't work. When we receive an intuitive prompting, it's usually simpler to follow it. The rewards are more beneficial than the consequences of resisting.

OUTER SPACE AND SUBTLE ENERGY

There is a story of a traditional Japanese gardener who was hired from Japan to create a garden in the grounds of a government building in Ottawa, Ontario. He arrived and looked over the bare land left by the construction, the land that was to become the garden. He turned to his employer and asked that he have access to a large field where he could collect natural rocks to use in the design of the garden.

His employer phoned a farmer he knew just outside of town and asked if the gardener could come and collect rocks. The farmer was clearing a new field and he offered to put all the rocks in a single pile so the gardener would have an easier time of choosing which ones he wanted to use. When the gardener arrived at the field he looked at the large pile of rocks, shook his head and began to walk out across the field gathering what rocks were left on the surface.

"Why did you do that?" his employer asked.

"Because the relationship between the rocks had been disrupted when they were moved into that great pile. They were no longer of any use in creating harmony in this garden. So I collected ones where I knew their relationship to each other so that I would be able to maintain the correct placement in the art of the garden."

We are like the rocks out of place, out of right relationship with each other, ourselves and our natural world, out of balance and without harmony.

Not knowing where to turn to learn more about aspects of interconnection in our relational world and our relationship with our environment, I kept reading any book I could find that might help me understand how to achieve more balance and harmony.

I met Brian just after my shamanic initiation on Cortes Island. I had heard about him at a meeting for chronic fatigue suffers, where they were discussing the possible environmental causes of that condition, factors such as electromagnetic radiation, geopathic stress and residual energy. The people in the group had experienced some relief after having their houses "cleared" and the "energy balanced." This sounded intriguing to me and since I was still suffering from very low energy I decided to give him a call. While I had recovered enough to stay up for the whole day, I didn't have enough energy to undertake anything but the simplest tasks. Malcolm was wonderful during this time — supportive and encouraging so that healing could take place.

After taking notes on the history of our house, and Malcolm's and my health concerns, Brian used kinesiology or muscle testing to confirm his sense of what was happening with the subtle environmental energy. To be muscle tested I would hold my arm at shoulder height and resist his gentle pressure downward. However, when he touched my forehead and the middle of my back, my arm went completely weak and he could push it down without effort. He explained that negative environmental energies affect various organ systems in our bodies and this was one way to verify what was happening energetically.

Many physiotherapists incorporate this technique into the examination of their patients to decide on the method of treatment.

Using observation, intuition, and imagination in combination with an eclectic array of tools including dowsing rods, pendulums, Black Hat Sect Feng Shui and compass directions, Brian opened a world just beyond the visible where energy and intention work together to create greater harmony and balance.

He began walking through the house with his right hand held about shoulder height. As he walked, his hand would move up and down as if running along the surface of some invisible field. Sometimes it would be as high as his head, sometimes down to his knees. He walked through our entire house doing this strange maneuver and then placed four small crystals of a kind of quartz called aventurine in specific corners at the front and back of the house. This seemed to flatten the surface that he had been following. Malcolm and I followed his path, exchanging quizzical glances, as if to say, "What on Earth is he doing?"

An outside observer would have developed some interesting theories, given the arm gyrations and hand waving taking place that afternoon. Much of Brian's work was based on an intuitive understanding of the flow of energy, or *ch'i*, and the consequences of the harmony or disharmony in the movement of *ch'i*.

The mysterious journey continued outside, with Brian making many suggestions about how we could improve the energy flow to our front door, called the Mouth of *Ch'i*, and attract more beneficial *ch'i* into the house and thus into our lives.

Brian worked from the principle that our houses are a reflection of our inner environment, and serve as metaphors for our experience. They provide us with an opportunity for insight into our inner selves and, through subtle changes, for energizing both our inner and outer worlds in harmony. As he moved through our house he explained the ideas of Feng Shui, which teach us how to work with our surroundings to implement enhancements that lead to beneficial change.

Black Hat Sect Feng Shui maps the energy centers of a house, using the *ba-gua* map, to distinguish areas that relate to the Nine

Life Endeavours of career, helpful people, travel, children, relationships, fame and recognition, wealth, family and knowledge.

I wanted to move back into environmental work to supplement what I could earn doing psychic readings. Using a *ba-gua* map as a guide we discussed ways to energize the "career area" in each room with simple decorating techniques.

After Brian completed his work we noticed that the house felt lighter and somehow more spacious and settled. Sitting at the kitchen table we talked about his background as a geomancer and his insights into the subtle energy that flows through our world and its effect on our health and well-being. Talk about geomancy, divination by means of the Earth, was fascinating. As a child in Hawaii I'd known of the Earth energies that the Goddess Pele commanded and how the Hawaiians held the energy of the Earth as sacred.

Each culture has had a geomantic tradition but most have lost the full body of this knowledge over the centuries. From the placement of the pyramids in Egypt to the temples at Chichen Itza in Mexico to the standing stones in Europe, we have little idea of the cultural understanding that placed these buildings in their particular relation to the heavens and the Earth, although we can have an appreciation of the breadth and depth of knowledge that must have been extant at the time.

The selection of favorable energetic sites for the construction of temples, palaces, homes and businesses was and, in many parts of the world still is, assisted by the knowledge of these earth energy patterns. This was a body of ancient knowledge about the Earth and how it works, about the interaction and interconnection of an energy found in all things, about using geomancy for insight to effect change and healing in ourselves and our environment.

Brian explained further the idea that our outer conscious reality, our home for example, reflects our inner unconscious reality. This made sense to me since I had read the work of Carl Jung and other leaders in the field of psychology, and researchers exploring the evolution of consciousness. I knew that the people and things around us reflect aspects of "who we are" and let us

139

see something of our interior persona, almost like looking into a psychic mirror. Here was a physical expression of the psychic paradigm that I had been exploring.

Brian wanted to write a book but didn't have the skill or computer equipment to do this. Having seen my computer system he proposed an exchange. He would provide me with training in the subtle energies of our environment as he understood them, in return for my typing and editing his book. Opportunity had entered our home and was sitting at the kitchen table.

I spent more than a year as an apprentice to Brian, as well as working on his book. The training was comprehensive and Brian taught me a language to describe what I was feeling and sensing in the environment. He helped me combine my intuitive skills and visual imagination with observation, to open my eyes further to this invisible world of energy. He provided a framework that gave an explanation for the imbalance and the tension I was sensing psychically in the physical world, and taught me the techniques to unblock, harmonize and balance the polarities.

His offer gave me an opportunity to incorporate my scientific training in ecology and anthropology into the metaphysical world of subtle energy, using tools from Feng Shui and shamanism. Now I could apply the skills of psychometry and remote viewing I had learned working as a psychic.

My first assignment with Brian involved choosing 12 houses and 12 offices, describing my direct experience of these places — how they "felt," what I sensed about them both inside and out and what I could gather about the emotional and physical health of the residents. I spent days sitting outside the houses, across the street, trying to get a sense of the energy of each one.

One house felt scared, another confused, and a third dark and depressed. A fourth felt hidden. I didn't know at that time what clues I was using to determine these conditions: I just sensed the houses in much the same way as I scanned people. I wondered how a house could feel hidden, or confused.

The next week Brian and I drove to each house and as we sat in my car we discussed what I had identified. As he began to help me express what I had experienced, he also pointed out features on the lot or roadway, which would lead to those feelings.

For example, the house that felt scared was at the end of a T-intersection, situated so that the traffic was pointed directly at the house before it turned either right or left. This house had poor boundaries, with no fence or trees to give it protection from the oncoming traffic, although to the logical brain there was no danger. The residents of the house, on a very subtle level, would have an underlying anxiety and find it difficult to relax.

We talked about the feeling in houses and where it came from, oppressive and dark, joyful and light, damp and stagnant, angry, spiky and agitated, and about ways to alleviate these conditions. This was geomancy at the environmental level, re-establishing a harmonious balance.

Once I had completed these assignments successfully, I was included in Brian's work with clients. I would accompany him to a house and observe what he did; then we would discuss it afterward over a cup of tea. Very much the apprentice, I had no role other than to observe and see if I could anticipate his actions and corrective measures, and learn the theory of this work.

In the homes and offices that we visited Brian used magnets and magnetic tape to neutralize electromagnetic radiation (EMR) from appliances and electrical outlets. He would use dowsing rods to locate zones of geopathic stress, and then he would place crystals, as he had in our home, to alleviate the effects. These stressful effects on human health are caused by abnormal energy fields generated within the earth itself and associated with a particular geologic region or terrain; for example, excavating for a foundation disturbs the natural flow of groundwater. Large mineral deposits, such as quartz, and underground features, such as flowing streams, disrupted water or dried stream beds can affect the electromagnetic field in the overlying areas and cause irritation to the physical body.

I remember the first house that we went to. The woman who lived there experienced debilitating headaches and had difficulty maintaining a high level of energy; it was as if her energy would somehow drain away unexpectedly. As I walked up the sidewalk

141

to the front door, I felt a change in the energy from the light and easy flow of a bright summer day to a thick, dense fog that was difficult to move through psychically. As Brian talked with the clients, Dave and Sue, I attempted to walk through the dining room. The fog coalesced into an overwhelming sense of pain, agony and grief in the room, particularly in one spot.

As Brian applied the magnetic tape to neutralize the EMR, and placed crystals to alleviate the geopathic stress, I investigated this thick energy psychically. I had a sense of someone lying in bed in the room. I was puzzled by this. It made no logical sense; there was no indication of anything other than a traditional dining room. All of the clearing that Brian usually did as a matter of routine had no effect on the energy of this room.

Brian noticed my difficulty and asked me what I was experiencing and where. After I described what I had sensed from the time I entered the house, Dave told us the story of his first wife who had lain for weeks in a special hospital bed in the dining room, wracked with pain from inoperable cancer. She enjoyed sitting in a recliner chair looking out the window, even though she could barely move. She sat in that chair for three days as she died, in the exact spot I had identified.

Brian decided it was time for me to practise some of the techniques he had taught me so he asked me to clear the dining room using the Planting Tree Visualization. This involved psychically planting trees in the room and calling the bright sun and clear rain to aid them to grow and bring in healthy and lush energy.

Standing there in the middle of the dining room I thought, "Okay, now what kind of tree shall I plant?" I decided that with the intensity of the grief, it ought to be a large tree, like a mighty sequoia. However, what I saw was a little acorn.

So I visualized planting acorns and oak trees around the dining room. When I was finished I came back to the present and described what I had done. Dave smiled widely as he told us that his deceased wife loved oak trees beyond all other kinds.

I went outside and stood on the grass doing a variety of clearing techniques to release any negative energy that I might have picked up in the dining room. I was gazing at the house and began to perceive a middle-aged woman on the front porch looking somewhat lost. I caught her attention and directed it to a brilliant light that had just appeared above the side of the house. She seemed unsure, so I extended my hand psychically and helped her walk toward it. At the last moment, before she walked through the gateway into the light, she turned and smiled. I finished clearing and went back into the house. It felt clear and empty. My description of the woman I had seen fit Dave's first wife, before she became ill.

Both Dave and Sue remarked that the house had never felt so open and light. Sue's headaches were much reduced in severity and her energy improved. It wasn't a perfect recovery, since there are other factors operating in illness and disease besides environmental ones, but it was a considerable improvement.

Residual energy, as in this case and that of the house that felt angry, is energy that is imprinted, and stuck in this space/time continuum. It is often the result of intense emotion affecting people in various ways, long after the event is over. Brian discovered that the people who had owned the angry house were embroiled in a vicious and nasty divorce action. Apparently the anger remained from their fights before the divorce.

Flying to Vancouver in a small commuter aircraft one day I became very uneasy for no apparent reason. It continued until I left the plane. I mentioned it to Brian later in the week and he said that it was possible that the person who had sat in the seat before me was intensely afraid of flying. That energy would cling to the seat and affect anyone who sat there, on a subtle level.

Brian explained that sometimes a house feels dark and depressing, and visiting there will leave a person feeling drained and headachy. The most serious locations for this residual energy are the spots in a park or on the street where violence has taken place. These will remain uncomfortable to sensitive people for a long time, unless they are cleared. Brian would often gather his students together and harmonize and clear the energy of the areas where violence had occurred.

The mystery of this work and this energy fascinated me. I began to get the idea that we were working with powers and

143

insights much greater than my analytical mind could comprehend. The sense of the spirit of a house, the spirit of place, of the people who had lived there and who presently live there, of the land on which it was built, was something that I began to treat with respect and awe. I had the feeling that we were privileged to catch a glimpse, however dimly, of a sacred world.

Negative emotional energy can also have a dramatic effect as I learned when Brian and I went to a site for a new home. Kathy and her husband invited us out to go over the architectural plans before the house was built so that Brian could make suggestions about the energy flow. He used pendulum dowsing to discern stagnant areas, or areas where the energy rushed too fast. The stairs were in line with the front door, allowing all the wealth to rush down the stairs and out the door, so he suggested a curving staircase, which Kathy agreed to.

A few months later, Kathy was running into all sorts of problems in the construction of her home. At each step of the way, difficulties would arise, necessitating more time and money. She asked for Brian's help, wondering why the problems were happening. Before we left town Brian asked me to check the site remotely. All I picked up was that a spirit was incredibly unhappy and didn't want the house built. I thought it might be related to the fact that this had been Indian land and perhaps the correct rituals and thanksgiving had not been performed.

Later, during the drive to the site, Kathy told us that the next-door neighbor was unhappy about the building of their house. He was concerned that it would block his view and have an impact on the quality of his life. Each time Kathy went to the site he would appear and tell her, in no uncertain terms, just how angry he was and how he didn't want their house built.

We walked around the site and could see that the neighbor's house overlooked her lot, so that each time he glanced out his window, he would see the offending construction site. Kathy, Brian and I psychically planted trees along the lot line, large trees that would provide a boundary between the two houses. Brian also used prayers of blessing and thanks to lift up the energy of the site.

It had begun to drizzle on the cloudy autumn day while we were standing by the corner of the lot talking about our experience. We heard the patio door open on the house next door, yet none of us looked, expecting an angry blast from the owner. However, his wife called out that since it was such a damp day, she and her husband would like to invite us in for tea.

Standing in the mud of that construction site on the side of a hill, with rain drizzling down from the low grey clouds, our eyes met in looks of awe.

"Amazing. I wouldn't have believed it possible," whispered Kathy.

The truth of Serge King's comment in his book *Earth Energies*, "The universe rearranges itself to accommodate our pictures of reality,"[5] was demonstrated to me that day quite dramatically. The building of Kathy's house proceeded smoothly to completion.

These experiences added to my growing awareness of the interconnectedness of all things, a connection of very subtle energy that can be altered by our thoughts alone. The results can be dramatic and often immediate. There might still be work to do on the physical plane, as in Kathy's need to establish a positive relationship with her neighbors, but the subtle pathway had been created — if she chose to walk that route.

My first opportunity to do a consultation on my own was for a friend who had a massage business in his home. He did a form of intense, deep-tissue massage but his business was not as successful as he wanted; clients were not coming quickly. His partner was working on her doctorate at the university and she had just found out that there would be no courses for her to teach that semester. It looked bleak financially. Burton called me to see if I could suggest anything. I drove out to their home by the ocean and could see immediately that, as you stood on the road, it was difficult to find their front door because the yard and walkway were overgrown with bushes.

Standing at the end of the walkway I could look right through their house and out through the picture window to the ocean. Pretty, but the energy that found their front door would continue on, right through the house and out the window. It is beneficial to have *ch'i* circulate through the home, and spiral in the center of rooms that are important to the family. This creates an energy vortex, which will attract more energy, rather than the stagnation of no flow. As I walked through the yard and house with Burton and his partner, I suggested simple changes like windsocks, candles or centerpieces that they could use to try to improve the energy flow and keep it in the house. Burton considered the weekend of yard work that would open up the path to his front door with dismay.

Within two weeks he had more clients than he could fit in and two new courses had turned up for his partner to teach. As Burton put it, "As strange as it seems, I have to credit the work that you suggested on our house for these changes. We did nothing different and our lives have shifted dramatically."

Usually after a consultation was finished, I would scan the house psychically one last time while I asked the question, "Was anything left undone?" There was quite a surprise waiting for me as I completed a consultation in a wonderful character home in an older section of town. Scanning the home, I could sense an area just behind one wall where there was a dark spot of something needing attention. I didn't know if it was residual energy or perhaps a high level of electromagnetic radiation. I walked through the house in an attempt to get to the spot and ended up in a bathroom. Opening the shower stall door revealed a pile of dirty clothes, the laundry of the last week that had been left undone. The owners and I had a good laugh at the discovery and the literal nature of our minds when they interpret the questions that we ask.

While I was working with Linda and her sister Millie in her house in California, we moved her sofa in an effort to eliminate the stagnant energy in her living room. As we moved the sofa about three inches, all of us heard an audible click and then felt the *ch'i* begin to move in the room, as if some gear had been engaged. We looked at each other in amazement. The room felt lighter and airier and it went from being seldom used to the family's favorite.

146

I began traveling to Southern California more frequently, after my marriage to Malcolm had ended, our house was sold, and my sons were settled at school. It was a wonderful relief to be traveling again after six years of staying in one place. Now my skills were completely portable and enabled me to travel widely.

These trips provided me with an opportunity to meet interesting people, work with homes that were quite different in structure and style from the ones on Vancouver Island, and give workshops on subjects like clutter and abundance from the perspective of Feng Shui.

Deborah was a small woman with an air of sadness around her. She had called me to ask for a consultation, when she couldn't attend my workshop on clutter, and driving up to her home, on a curving street on the side of a hill, I began to get a sense of the stagnant and stuck energy she had mentioned over the phone.

She had commented that her house was full of clutter, and that she felt tired and lacked motivation. Also, she mentioned that she was suffering from digestive and colon problems. Often, when our lives are filled with the clutter of old and worn-out things or beliefs, there is no space for new joys and blessings to enter, no way for the subtle *ch'i* to flow.

As I drove into her driveway I noticed a "blocking" tree, a very large and healthy citrus that prevented the front windows from receiving any light, and grew over the roof of the house. Deborah greeted me at the door and invited me into the living room. One of the first things I noticed was a lack of clutter. Everything was neat and tidy, without the usual piles of paper or miscellaneous objects usually associated with the idea of clutter. All the window shades were drawn and closed, giving the interior space a dark, cave-like appearance.

We chatted for a few moments and then moved to the kitchen. This room was filled with light from an uncurtained window, the only one in the house. We sat at the kitchen table and I began to ask the questions that would enable me to get a sense of her needs and wishes with respect to the consultation.

Her husband had died five years previously, after a lengthy illness at home. The house was exactly as it had been when he became ill; his desk still had his pencils scattered about. His death had left Deborah completely at a loss about how to continue on as a single woman. She had only two good friends and no family. Her biggest desire was to move forward and build a new life for herself, to bring in friendly people who would be fun to be around and who would be able to help her if it was needed.

We decided to enhance the helpful people area in her bedroom. As I sat on her bed I noticed that her husband's hat and night things were still in plain view. The top of the dresser at the foot of the bed held photographs of a number of people, and several of a cat. I inquired about those.

Deborah began to describe their cat. Since they had had no children, this cat had filled a very important place in their lives for 17 years. Beside the picture was an urn that held the ashes of the cat. One photo was of her aunt who had died of breast cancer, another of her grandmother who had passed away from a stroke. Yet another was of her husband holding their cat in happier times. There were no pictures of people who were still alive. Deborah saw the benefit of moving all these pictures out of her bedroom into the ancestor area in her living room as indicated in the *ba-gua* map.

In each room she commented on the lack of friends in her life. As we sat at her kitchen table, she spoke of the difficulty of carrying on alone. While I listened to her, my lungs began to burn quite painfully. "Now what?" I wondered. Then my throat started to hurt, especially on swallowing.

I wondered if I had caught some virus, although I had a sense that this was not a case of instant flu. A similar experience some months before had been because of a departed spirit that wished to make its presence known to my client. My throat was rapidly worsening and I began to cough. The coughing intensified until I felt as though I had a small hole in my throat that was being irritated. As the symptoms continued to worsen and Deborah went to get a glass of water, I realized I wasn't getting the message.

An image of my friend and psychic, Joyce, came to mind. She is a medium who channels departed spirits, and I've watched her as she was channeling. She experienced the symptoms of the cause of death in order to give a verifiable clue to her client about who their guardian angel was.

The light dawned! I asked Deborah if anyone around her had died of lung and throat problems.

"No," she replied, "I can't think of anyone." Her face reflected her bewilderment. "Oh yes, yes, there was someone, my grandfather! He had TB. He continued to smoke and developed lung cancer. Even after they removed part of his lung he continued to smoke until he developed throat cancer and they did a tracheotomy. He finally died gasping for breath."

"It appears that your grandfather is here as your guardian angel and as a helpful person to guide you through the task of clearing out your home and building a new life."

"I never really knew him when he was alive. Why would he help me?"

I could hear her grandfather saying that he wished that it had been different when he was alive and now he was pleased to be able to help from the other side. I shared this with Deborah. We chatted about addictions and other aspects of living that she could see in the story of her grandfather and also in her own life.

My visit to California this time seemed to be about clearing residual energy, whether it was Deborah's home or in the Mantras School. This was an alternative school that ran from kindergarten to Grade Twelve. The school was in an old mission building close to a Native graveyard. Ever since they had moved into the building, the students had been more unsettled and disruptive than they had been in the previous location. I was visiting the school with a friend, Cheryl, whose daughter attended Grade Five.

The subtle energy was flowing reasonably well, although it had a decided undercurrent of sadness and anguish. Cheryl also worked with subtle energy as a healer and we often shared experiences and insights about the creative process of encountering and working with this energy. I suggested that we do a short

149

clearing ritual to see if we could shift the energy onto a more positive note.

I described the Planting Tree Visualization. She caught on quickly and added her own style and intention to the method. She had an excellent foundation for working with energy, and she knew the principle that our intention was more important than the form that we used in this creative process. I trusted her judgment completely about what was needed for the highest good.

We sat quietly for about 20 minutes working with this energy psychically through the visualization. We walked outside into the sunshine for a few moments to clear our energy field and then went back into the school to pick up her daughter. We met the director of the school who asked us about the shift in energy that she had noticed just a few moments before. It felt much lighter and warmer in her office now. Cheryl called me a couple of days later to tell me that the children had settled down; they were focussing much better and seemed happier to be at their desks.

The residual energy in this building was both from the aboriginal land underneath the structure and from the brutal history of conflict between the Church and the aboriginal population. The proximity of the graveyard also played a role, as did some sad and tragic events that had occurred in a residential school that had once been housed in the building. This experience made it eminently clear again, that our behavior and sense of well-being are directly affected by the subtle energies in our environment on the very deepest level.

This was confirmed as I drove down the coast to Ventura for a leisurely sightseeing trip. I reached San Luis Obispo about mid-afternoon, feeling wonderfully carefree and happy. As I drove along the main street leading into town I had the sense of passing through a wall of powerful energy, so strong it took my breath away for a moment. Then I noticed my mood turning very dark and angry. All of a sudden I was frustrated by the traffic, feeling impatient and trapped.

"My God, what happened," I wondered.

The shift had been as quick as a breath. As I drove on, the angry and impatient feelings settled into my body. Somehow, I was rapidly adapting to the energetic climate of this area and no longer noticing it as something unusual.

The surroundings seemed charming, the houses neat and well-cared for. Yet the anger grew in intensity. As I turned a corner onto the street leading out of town I noticed a sign saying "California Men's Colony."

How odd, I thought, that here is a huge building as a retreat or colony only for men. It took a few moments to dawn on me. This was the California state penal colony, a maximum-security prison. That explained the energy field!

About two miles farther down the road I drove through another energy wall and all of a sudden the day was bright and sunny, my mood had lightened considerably.

Here was a circle about four miles across filled with the brutal and destructive energy of the people who were imprisoned there! What must it be like to live within that circle? How would it affect the lives of those people, even if they had no direct contact with the prison?

It had been a dramatic shift for me, and yet I realized how quickly I adapted to the overwhelming feelings and how soon they became nothing unusual. What about the children growing up in that energy field? How would they be influenced? And how strong do people need to be in order to maintain their integrity and sense of self within such an energy field?

I had no answers. Certainly there would have been a subtle yet profound effect, especially over time. The best I could think of then was to ensure that my own energy field and that of my home and surrounding area were as positive and clear as possible.

Brian had spoken of a number of methods for clearing space, such as smudging, burning sage in a room to transform the negative energy; sweeping the room, including the ceiling, with a fresh cedar bough, just like dusting; or keeping a bowl of clean water with sea salt to absorb the disruptive energy. Generally I tried to smudge my house with sage or sweetgrass every other day, more frequently if there were a lot of negative things happening, like light bulbs burning out or appliances breaking; these are sure signs that the space needs cleansing.

Subtle environmental energy that is unseen, yet felt and experienced, is a significant part of our daily world. We respond to it from moment to moment, even if we are unaware of its existence. This "power of place" can result in a shift in our mood, sometimes slight, other times dramatic. We adjust so quickly, being the most adaptable species on the planet, that we are often unaware of the change until some time later when we are left wondering what happened and why our day changed in such a way.

TWEAKS

Having just returned from a trip to California, my first order of business was to check my phone messages. This was usually a simple procedure of dialing a special number and entering the password to my mailbox when I heard the voice prompt. This time, though, I couldn't seem to get through. I dialed the sequence and heard a voice prompt saying that it was incorrect. So I entered it again, and heard the same prompt. And I entered it again, thinking I had hit the wrong key on my small phone pad.

About this time I noticed a very soft and quiet voice saying "star" somewhere in my consciousness. I noticed it, but didn't pay attention to it. I heard the phone prompt again, telling me I had entered an incorrect password. So I entered the sequence again, this time in that very deliberate way that we use when we're reaching a certain level of frustration. I heard the same voice prompt from the phone and a somewhat louder "star" from the ether.

I dialed the sequence again, even more deliberately. When I heard the voice prompt this time I thought there must be something wrong with the phone pad. Absolutely determined to retrieve my messages, I looked at the phone and began to enter the sequence again, muttering, "What on Earth is the matter with this phone service?" This time I heard "star" as an audible shout over and over, just as loud as the automated voice coming from the phone. It was loud enough to get my attention this time.

152

"Star?" I thought. "Star??" And the light dawned. I had been pressing the pound key rather than the star key. This was the single difference necessary for retrieving messages from in or out of the country. Having finally heard that correct prompt, I entered the sequence using "star" and immediately got in to my mailbox.

This was a small event in the whole context of my day; however, I would have saved myself much aggravation if I had paid attention to my internal prompting, rather than to the one from the phone. The phone was telling me that I couldn't achieve my goal, rather than what to do to have a successful outcome, which is always the purpose of that still, small voice inside.

Clearly, I was set on what I thought was the right path to achieving my goal, and was so determined to follow it, repeating it almost endlessly, that I was unable to hear or see any other way. I wondered, in those moments after this experience, how often this happens in the busy and noisy turmoil of our everyday lives and how much easier life would be if we followed our internal prompting rather than reacting to the external ones. I wondered, and I finally decided to pay attention.

As if to test my commitment, the next day I was sitting in the office of the principal of my son's new school. Walter, the principal, and I had developed a friendship during the time Devin had attended the school and we were having a meeting about Aiden's classes for the coming year. We chatted about what would be best and how well he might succeed at this school.

"Now that we've talked about Aiden, tell me what you can see for the school in this term." Walter was fascinated by the psychic realm and had attended many meetings about power spots and sacred sites. He had called me previously to do an energy assessment of the school, hoping to find ways to calm the frenetic activity of 300 teenagers. Now he wanted some insight into what might face him over the next few months.

I thought about what he had asked and fear surfaced. I remembered my commitment to listen and pay attention, and to move beyond my reluctance.

153

"First, there's going to be trouble down at that corner of the school," I said as I pointed over to the cafeteria. "It's going to happen outside at ground level and it will disrupt the school badly. I can't see exactly what happens though."

We talked about what it might be, since that was the storage area for the school. Perhaps there would be a water leak or the freezer would break.

"And then something is going to happen over there in the science block, in the lab. Nothing serious but it's going to disrupt the classes."

Again we talked about what this event might be. There were two science teachers, one very stable and practical, the other somewhat emotional and easily troubled. Walter thought that the second teacher might need stress leave at some point during the year.

"The worst event, though, is going to happen in your house and will affect you personally. I see you sitting beside your phone waiting anxiously for a phone call and praying everything will be okay. And it looks like it will be."

We both had to continue with the schedule of our day so I left Walter deep in thought, wondering about what was going to happen in each of these scenarios. I was curious about how that information had surfaced, how accurate it was.

I saw Walter at school about two months later. He was smiling as he walked up to me. "You're scary!" he said.

What did I do now, I wondered, having completely forgotten about our discussion.

"It was the garbage truck," Walter said. "The driver lifted the dumpster too high and took out all the electrical lines and phone lines running into the school. He's been doing this route for 15 years and has no idea what happened. But it put the school into chaos for two days. We were just in the middle of completing registration and timetabling. It was a terrible mess.

"You pegged the problem in the science block too. My best and most stable teacher has had to take a six-month leave to go to England for family reasons. His father had a serious stroke and had to be put into a care facility. As a result, all the family

154

affairs needed to be straightened out. So he's gone and it's really affecting the school.

"Do you still get a sense of the third thing? The event in my house with me sitting by the phone?"

Without thinking, I scanned into the future and could still see the event happening. "Yes, I can, although I don't see it any more clearly. It has something to do with family rather than the school itself and it appears to turn out well."

I saw Walter again at the Christmas concert. He walked up to me with a serious look. "You were right. My wife went in for an emergency operation two weeks ago in the middle of the night, and there I was, sitting by the phone, waiting for the call to let me know that the operation was a success. She's recovering well and should be back to herself by Christmas."

Thankful that his wife was home and healing, I wished Walter a Merry Christmas and went home to wonder.

At what point are future events decided? It seems it must be some time before they happen but when? And could we change them if we had some foresight?

Where does this energy come from, I wondered. How does it swirl through our lives? What is this profound mystery that animates our world? I could appreciate it as part of our physical environment, but there was something else, some other, more intangible source of influence.

One day I was sitting at my desk, writing out cheques to pay my bills, when I felt a tweak. That's the only way I can describe it — a tweak somewhere in my energy field. It was like the blink of an eye, and ever so subtle. Just a tweak, a nudge, that could easily go unnoticed.

First there was the tweak, then my hand reached for the phone, unbidden by my conscious awareness. I watched it move across my desk to lift the receiver almost of its own accord. As my hand lifted the receiver I thought, "Phone Paul now." And with that thought, I dialed. It was more a command than a thought.

Paul was a good friend who had coached me on some business dealings. I hadn't talked to him for months. His answering machine responded and as I was in the middle of leaving a brief message to have him call me, Paul lifted up the phone and answered with, "All right, Dy, that's too weird for me. As I stepped through my front door, just a moment ago, I thought of you, and thought I needed to talk to you. And with that thought, my phone rang, and it's you calling me! That's too weird."

He wanted to ask for my psychic insight into some financial problems that he was having, and my reading on future possibilities, and we chatted for a few minutes. It was the tweak of a thought directed my way that I had caught as it went past.

Maybe it's more like James Lovelock's Gaia hypothesis than I realized. Lovelock saw the energy of our planet, which he termed Gaia, like a web, a gigantic spider web of connection that runs out from our center to all the people and things in our world. It's an energetic matrix that serves as a conduit for information among the threads of our existence, always leading back to center, our center, the center of our being, the center of our planet.

CHAPTER NINE

MYSTERY AND WONDER: THOUGHTS ALONG THE WAY

So WHY DID I write this book and what have I learned from all this?

My direct experiences with being psychic have led me into an awareness and appreciation of the subtle energies of the natural world around us, energies that can be felt, seen and worked with. In part, this book emerged from my hope to provide some beacons and lights for others traveling along this path to awakening. In large part though, the "why" came from the encouragement and persistence of Beth Hill and from the direction given by my guides during the following shamanic journey.

I was with my friend Anna at her home on the outskirts of Victoria one July afternoon. Her house was located at the end of a valley between two green and wooded hills, hills that funneled wind and good weather to nurture her garden and bring her messages from the wind spirits.

Anna, whom I had met at a psychic fair, was from Eastern Europe, trained by Michael Harner and Sandra Ingerman, of the

Institute for Shamanic Studies, in the ways of the ancient art of shamanic journey and soul retrieval. That afternoon Anna was to lead me on a journey, one that would influence the course of my life far into my future.

As I drove up to her white, Spanish-style house, I was filled with apprehension, not about taking the journey, which was something I had done many times before, particularly after my shamanic training and initiation, but about what information I would receive from the spirits of the Upper World. My past experience told me that the information received was always transformative, leading to changes in a person's life and way of being in the world. I knew these journeys were not to be undertaken lightly.

Anna and I greeted each other warmly and walked to her sacred space. Her home was decorated with a wonderful and eclectic collection of masks from various cultures around the world: the Inuit of the Arctic, the First Nations peoples of the Four Corners region, and many from Africa and Bali.

Once settled on comfortable futons draped with heavy, earth-colored fabric, we chatted about the new events in our lives and decided on the length of time for the journey. The butterflies were dancing in my stomach as we drank our tea.

With the last sip from her cup, Anna arose and reached for her spirit rattle, a beautiful piece made from deer hide dyed an intense shade of turquoise, with a carved bone handle. Feathers, claws and ribbons dangled from the handle and their movement deepened the sound of the rattle itself.

In preparation, I lay down, closed my eyes and made myself comfortable on the rug. I had fasted for 24 hours and completed cleansing rituals in preparation. Now was the moment to begin the journey.

Anna began to shake her rattle to clear the space of any negative energy and to call in our spirit helpers and guides. The energy in the room was electrified, as the rattling grew louder and more intense. Abruptly she stopped, picked up her shaman's drum and began the rhythm of the heartbeat. She would drum for me while I journeyed to the Upper World, seeking answers to my questions about the next six months. Shamanic journeys like this one are often done when people are seeking deeper answers to questions about the direction of their lives.

Slowly I began to see a forest path leading through dense fir trees to an open meadow. The sun was shining and off in the distance I could make out mountains and valleys. It was much like a dream, but a dream in which you know you are awake and dreaming in your sleep at the same time. Walking through the meadow I could feel myself move farther and farther away from Anna's room and farther into the Middle World. The meadow was filled with wildflowers, yellow buttercups and white daisies and blue cornflowers sprinkled through the grass. The wind whispered on my skin as it gently moved the tall meadow grass. The edge of a cliff was appearing at the end of the meadow. I thought, "No way am I going to jump off that cliff."

The visualizations of my journeys often included the sense of jumping off cliffs, in effect jumping into the unknown, something I struggled with in my everyday life. I'm often reluctant to move without knowing just where I'm going. I stood at the edge of that cliff, took a deep breath and leaped.

Not afraid in this metaphysical world, I knew that I journeyed with spirits much wiser than I was. I had often sensed their presence and seen their forms as I moved through other worlds. Anna's instructions had been clear though: "Get to the Upper World any way you can and ask whoever you meet what you need to do for yourself during the next six months." So I knew I had to rise from the Middle World somehow. I would have preferred climbing a tree or rope ladder.

As I fell, my stomach came up into my throat as if I was on the first big hill of a roller coaster, and then I was moving straight upward through the air at a rapid rate. I was always surprised when the events in a journey have an actual physical impact. There is obviously a very close connection between what happens in our minds and what our body experiences.

The air was clear with a few cotton clouds on the horizon, sunny and warm. As I rose farther I could see above me a green, transparent platform, like light green plastic. "Now what is that doing there?" I wondered.

159

My motion ceased as I came level with the platform and I stepped onto it. It seemed like the appropriate thing to do. Looking into the distance, I waited in anticipation for a spirit of the Upper World to appear.

In the distance a figure began slowly approaching. As he came closer his white robes, long white beard and bald head suggested the form of a Master. From his golden belt hung sacred geometric symbols made from various metals. He came up to me, held out both hands and looked deeply into my eyes. As I placed my hands in his, he said, "Welcome home."

I was stunned for a moment by the intensity of his welcome and by his startling amber eyes. As I looked at him I desperately tried to remember the question that I was supposed to ask. I wanted to get it exactly right, so that I would get the correct answer. I had a belief that we always received the answer that is for our highest good and evolution, even if it seems strange at the time.

"What am I supposed to do for myself for the next six months?"

And the Master replied, "Write."

"Right?" I echoed perplexed. Then I understood. "Write? How?"

He replied, "Like the wings of a bird." And with that a huge flock of white doves exploded across the azure sky in front of us.

Being one to want a lot of detailed instruction, I asked, "And what shall I write about?"

"Tell your story."

"Oh great," I thought. "Haven't I written enough about myself in the recovery and personal healing work that I've done?" Journaling had been an activity that was very helpful for self-exploration when I was healing my vision and low energy.

He continued, "Tell all that you know, for everyone to see. Tell the story of our soul and we will share with you more to write. Just write!"

That was pretty clear, even for me. He then held out a multi-colored pyramid so that I would know to purchase one like it, to help me in my writing. With that question out of the way, we walked together along the platform.

Anna began to sound the call back, a certain drum rhythm which alerts the journeyer that the time is ending. The Master and I walked to the edge of the platform. While we were standing there, I was hoping for a novel thought to indicate some way to get back down to the Middle World, other than jumping again.

As I was thinking, the Master gently cupped my head in his hands, so that I was looking into his golden amber eyes. He held my head so I could see that his eyes were merely colored veils. I was drawn in and through to the space behind his eyes where I began to see planets being created by his very thought. There were multiple universes beyond the form of his eyes and I swam through them in ecstasy. And then it was time to jump.

"Hold on," I thought, and then realized that I could not hold on in the Upper World. It is a place of letting go. I took a deep breath and stepped off the edge of the platform. As I tumbled down like a lead weight I head a voice in my head saying, "Remember your parachute." I reached around my shoulder, found a cord that I hadn't realized was there, pulled it and a brilliant red heart opened above my head. I floated gently back to the Middle World and then to the floor of Anna's sacred room.

And so a book was conceived and, with Beth's prompting during our trips together, this book on being psychic was fleshed out. Still reluctant, I was slow in starting the project until I had an unusual "accident" at the gym two months after the journey. It put me in a leg cast for eight weeks, so it was either focus on writing or watch daytime soap operas which wasn't an attractive alternative. Each time we talked Beth would ask about my progress and how many pages were written. There was nothing else to do but write.

***

"What have I learned from all this?" was a question I often asked. Most of us wonder at one time or another: what is my greater purpose here, why am I living the life that I have? We search for some reason for our lives, a reason that is more than just the sum total of all the decisions we have made. It seemed there must have been some reason for my explorations into the psychic realms, for my second sight, other than simply the luck of the draw. Here were the old questions of "Why me, God?" and "What now?"

Perhaps Gandhi's words express the answer best: "My life is my teaching." Life has taught me, and through these stories may provide ideas for others.

There is a psychic realm to explore that is beyond the separation of space and time, where we are deeply connected and aware, in harmony with all things — past, present, and future. If there is disharmony we find struggle and disease in our lives. It is a place where we can experience the unity of humanity with the Earth and all that is around us, a world based on the integration of duality. It is beyond individual ego, beyond personality, a system much larger than self, a place of sacred witness to the inherent goodness and integrity of the spirit in all life, be it mountain, forest or living creature.

What we call "psychic" is one expression of this expanded awareness, based on the willingness to explore beyond our limited beliefs into the uncharted waters of the "sea of consciousness," as it's been called. We begin by putting in one toe to test the water — broadening our capacity for empathy and intuition. Slowly, we move deeper into the sea through compassionate understanding and acknowledgment of synchronicity, serendipity and illusion. We expand consciously into a reality where space, time and separation are redefined.

There is a story in the Buddhist community about a lady who was intensely afraid of snakes. She went into her kitchen during the night to get a glass of water, and saw a huge snake coiled up on the floor. She ran from the room in terror. Her husband came to her rescue and turned on the kitchen light — to reveal a coiled rope lying beside the back door. She was no longer afraid. The question posed is this: "How can a snake that does not exist disappear when a light is turned on?"

Ramana, a Buddhist teacher in California, while leading a *satsang* or spiritual coming together that I attended, noted that we often consider the fear of death the deepest fear of mankind. Yet he considers that there are three deeper fears: that the person we trust the most will betray us; that the person we love the most will leave us; and that the thing we need the most will not be there at the moment that we need it.

Wondering about this story and Ramana's questions, I realized that much of my world had been defined by my fears, usually imaginary ones. I also knew that in this psychic realm where the energy of consciousness and clarity of thought shape the experience of our world, intention is of paramount importance. We can ask ourselves: "What do we intend to have happen in this situation? What is our desired outcome?" Often it's clear on the surface but the questions are more relevant, and more powerful, when asked spiritually.

Much of the philosophy that I follow suggests, with respect to fear and death, that when we stand without form in the formless, we do not cease to exist. We become who we truly are, pure energy, conscious and aware of our limitless universe. In this way of being fully in our bodies and completely focussed on the present, there is no separation through space or time. Illusion disappears and death becomes a change of vibration rather than an end to awareness.

Like so much in our world, attempts to communicate psychic experiences and interactions with the subtle energy around us are limited by our need to define what is inherently undefinable. We begin to use form to describe what appears intangible to our conscious minds: spirit guides, angels, starbeings, fate, chance, luck, for example. Descriptions, explanations and analysis seem to restrict our understanding rather than enhance it.

Working with any of the energy tools available today, like Feng Shui, accupressure, Reiki, magnetics, to name a few, it is possible to effect subtle change directly, in people, their lives, organizations and places, to unblock the flow, clear out stagnation and harmonize movement. Like taking debris out of a blocked stream, this clearing away restores the dynamic equilibrium of the natural system. Our own healing, through releasing habits and life stories which no longer serve for our growth,

163

doing inner work, and keeping our bodies as healthy as possible, assists in this clearing process. Deborah, in California, was a good example: movement forward in her life was blocked by the presence and clutter of all the things from her departed husband. More than psychological, this stagnation had an effect on her body in the form of digestive and colon disease.

Eastern thought sees this world as an expression of the energy of polarity. Rather than a world of opposites separate and distinct, like bright and dull, the world is comprised of unique energetic states that are not static but constantly changing into the next expression of energy. Polarity exists as a state of dynamic equilibrium; even a mountain, usually thought of as large, is becoming small as a result of erosion. In this way, light flows into dark which then flows into light in a constant circle of motion, like the Chinese symbol of yin and yang, the wholeness and balance of night plus day.

My experiences with remote viewing and psychic reading suggest a realm of no space, no geographical separation as we conceive it. Perhaps it's more like a world of vibration without form, that connects each one of us and all that comprises the Earth and heavens into a single matrix.

From that first workshop on Gabriola Island learning about remote viewing, to working on the psychic phone line, I had been struck by the apparent lack of any kind of absolute spatial separation. It was as easy to observe an address in Australia as it was to see the house across the street, once that skill and belief had developed. The mystery of this was intriguing. Geographic space seems to be a phenomenon that provides us the opportunity to experience a physical reality, a way of referencing our location relative to any other. This experience of separation, of "me" and "other" doesn't apply in the psychic environment.

As Brian Swimme, a quantum physicist who wrote *The Universe Story* with Thomas Berry, said in a lecture in Victoria, "If we had a telescope that allowed us on Earth to see the very, very farthest star in the universe, we would be looking at the back of our head." In this mass of energy, any point can be viewed from any other point in the matrix as an infinite loop or web of life.

Experiences with psychometry, residual energy and channeling suggest that there is no time, no temporal separation, either. It appears to be as easy to see events 20 minutes ago as 20 years ago. Perhaps the past, present, and future exist simultaneously in a kind of temporal spiral, a series of cycles within which we can view any moment in the spiral from any other moment.

Time becomes relative, and linear time is a malleable state, so that it can be compressed or extended according to our intention. We have all had the experience of time seeming to stand still, dragging, or speeding up. Certainly the passage of time appears to change radically in our experience, even though the chronometer may denote some exact finite measurement often unrelated to our direct experience. Yet there is also the experience of leaving late for an important appointment and arriving precisely at the designated moment, even though the usual amount of time required for the journey would have made us late. Sometimes the only plausible explanation is that time was somehow shifted.

The aboriginal concept of right time is one that fascinated me. This idea holds time as an opportunity rather than something read from a clock face: the right time to go hunting, the right time to go to sleep. When the time is right, events and decisions unfold easily and smoothly. If the timing is inappropriate or out of phase, events and decisions are a struggle and better left to another time. As Lee told us many times in the workshop on Gabriola, when it's right, it's effortless, whether it's loving another person or designing and completing a research project.

It appeared to me that we live in a physical world composed of subtle energy — of things vibrating with a unique signature which, at their core, have no inherent substance, merely vibration. Aspects of the psychic environment are comprised of these unique signatures which we name in order to give them form — hand, tree, ocean, wife.

With a certain level of consciousness and focus we can begin to escape the bonds of the space-time continuum and move in an unlimited manner, without the restrictions of perceptual space or time. Perhaps this is the transcendence of physical matter so often sought by the mystics and sages.

165

Remote health readings suggest that the form we hold is less dense than it appears, being comprised of an electromagnetic field and a vital energy source, our essence. All details of anatomy and psyche can be examined without the aid of X-ray machines or fluoroscopes and there is no need to be in the same room — or the same city!

Our physical bodies extend beyond a mechanistic model; more than a machine, they are the dynamic and living universe within which our soul resides. The "real" world extends beyond what we can see: smell and hearing are examples of tapping into levels of our world that are more faint than observable physical reality. Our body and soul in partnership exist within the greater universe in which we all live.

Intuitive medicine comes from the idea that disease has an energetic origin; it is caused when our energy is out of balance, blocked or stagnant. Traditional Western thought tends to examine the chemistry of our bodies and adjust it with drugs or therapy. Seldom does it examine, as Eastern thought does, the energy of our bodies, and balance that energy flow to achieve health. Through phenomena like the observer effect, and the research of medical intuitives like Carolyn Myss, it appears that "what we think" becomes "what we are."

Many esoteric disciplines teach of a subtle energy that flows through all things, animate and inanimate, known by many names such as *ch'i* (Chinese), *ki* (Japanese) and *prana* (Indian). Our conscious intent can influence this energy on many levels. The power of prayer in healing is now being taught in medical schools across the United States. Reiki Masters and practitioners are sending healing energy across long distances to those in need. The practice of Feng Shui and related disciplines is bringing home and office environments into energetic balance and harmony, leading to enhanced health for the residents.

Beyond the physical world of energy our lives are mythic experiences filled with the drama of story and symbol. Three stages of insight can be useful in discovering the story.

The first and most superficial level to observe is the physical structure of our lives: our families, our careers, our homes. For example, questions like "Are there lots of friends and family or is it a solitary life?" help us to begin to see the framework of our story.

A deeper level finds the metaphor, those symbols and signs that we use as representations for the meaning of our lives. Surrounding ourselves with the subtle energies of objects, pictures, and sounds that "speak to us," and act like a mirror of ourselves, we can see more clearly who we are as individuals and where we've come from on this journey. Are the things around us sensuous or austere? Colorful or drab?

Deeper still is the spirit of our lives, the purpose and passion that are the core energy of our creation, of our life story. Through ritual and ceremony, we bring this purpose into visible physical form. Moving our life into the sacred, becoming aware of sacredness around us, opens the possibility of direct communication with Spirit. Where is a sense of this sacred in your day?

***

Firewalks and remote viewing are only small examples of the infinite power of our minds. If we can harness this power, we can learn to employ it for growth and service, and for the good of humankind and our planet. As De la Warr realized in his experiments increasing crop yields, the human mind is the most vital factor. He demonstrated increases in yield of between 84% and 270%, even over distance, when plants or soil plots were treated with subtle energy focussed by the thought and the intention of the sender.

Evidence from other researchers like Mesmer in the 1700s, Reich and Reichenbach in the 1800s and 1900s and present day researchers like King and Myss, as well as experiences reported by others, indicate a subtle energy that, when honored, can assist and support us in our lives. When dishonored, it invites in a kind of entropy which can contribute to blocks, stagnation, unmet wants and expectations, anxiety, fear and ultimately disease. Environmental blocks like clutter and others examined by Feng Shui, along with emotional, physical and spiritual blocks, can wreak havoc in our lives and our world.

167

As we open psychically, we begin to become sensitive to our Earth's energy, and ride the ebb and flow of her cycles along with those of our moon. We live in a time of depleting resources on this Earth. We can look around and see the loss of species, of forest, of prairies, of wilderness. As we look inside we can see the energy depletion in people and their lives: lack of resources, financial and material, lack of work, loss of personal energy, a longing to find that which is missing. We are beginning to reflect Earth's depletion with our very bodies. Truly, the Microcosm reflects the Macrocosm, or said another way, what is outside is also inside, as Brian taught me so long ago.

The triangle of body-mind-spirit is expanding into the square of body-mind-spirit-environment. The first cure is to remove the clutter from our own "square." We remove all those things, ideas, beliefs and attitudes that no longer serve to bring joy. This creates an opening so that new joys and blessings can enter and it's easier to catch the whispers with open space around us. All those old and useless things take up physical and energetic space, and create stagnation.

Scientists are finding that what they considered the vacuum of space is really quite busy with the energy of movement. It is in the space between "things" that harmony and balance can occur. The space between objects holds light, the space between our words holds the energy of our intention, and the space between our thoughts is where we encounter our soul.

The quality of our relationships to things, the planet and each other defines and shapes our existence. The space in these relationships is our creative field where we work with the energy of "our thoughts, words, and deeds." In his book *The Quark and the Jaguar*, Murray Gell-Mann suggests that quantum physics and the scientific and medical communities are beginning to find that consciousness is the base of this subtle, all-pervasive energy. Researchers are discovering that energy can be modified and shifted through nothing more than an act of intention on the part of the individual working within the energy field, something that ancient cultures were aware of and utilized.

Having psychic skills is one possible stop along the pathway to developing our minds, our consciousness, to their fullest. With practice, using these skills becomes an integrated part of our awareness and our daily way of living. It's curious and intriguing at first, much like a fairground at the side of the road where we can stop and play for a while.

There is the roller-coaster ride of increasing sensitivity, the times of being overcome by others' perceptions or drained by another's neediness. It's easy to lose our sense of self in the Hall of Mirrors, the realm of projection, judgment and blame, externalizing our problems onto someone or something else. And then there is the merry-go-round, going round and round in circles, not knowing when or where to get off, or how to stop the whirlwind of this opening.

I have learned that psychic skills can be very helpful in living our lives, giving us a source of information far greater than anything our rational and logical minds can conceive. Psychic awareness provides access to a very powerful source, one that gives more grace and ease to living. Yet being psychic does not mean that one is enlightened, or even particularly bright.

The awareness of the psychic realm, of this expanded awareness, often begins with small things: faint sensations or blurred pictures, distant voices whispering. This allows a psychic or sacred connection to emerge with people and places on an intensely intimate level. It is the direct experience of the observer effect, in which our very presence, observation and expectation can change an outcome or affect the future in very subtle, yet profound ways. Part of the pathway for developing psychic awareness is to begin to recognize the subtleties, and build on them, practising and exercising this aspect of our being.

We as humans are inseparable energetically from this planet and all that exists here, a connection deeper even than our scientific thought would indicate. We are part of a vast system wherein all parts influence all other parts simultaneously. The coming time will lead us to integrate information and understanding about this universal energy into new solutions and previously unthought-of ways of doing things.

Considering the subtle energies around us and the problems we face on our planet today, a paraphrase of Einstein's observation seems relevant: A solution cannot be found through the same level of thinking as that which created the problem. When you think you've found the answer, go deeper into the question and then deeper still.

It remains a mystery to me why I was sensitive to this realm of subtle energy and open to psychic abilities from a very early age. I have wondered how they came so naturally into my life, despite my unwillingness, and continued to come despite my stubborn reluctance. Slowly I have learned to work with them, to honor them and to be thankful for them.

This opportunity to see beyond what we normally perceive is open to all of us. I believe it is our birthright and natural way of being as a species. It can be re-awakened through a willingness to participate in something larger than one's self.

Another key to gaining psychic skills is something my father used to say to me about any new skill I was learning: "Practise, practise, practise." Begin with creating parking spaces, discerning who is on the phone before you answer; ask of your psychic perception, "what is the right thing to do, the right thing to buy and which store has it." I used to stand at the produce counter in the grocery store and practise choosing the sweetest fruit or the ones with the thinnest peel, for example. Then I would buy the fruit and check how accurate I was. It made the monotony of grocery shopping more fun and interesting.

I encourage you to explore this realm, to play and have fun with the ideas presented here and most of all to observe your own direct experience. Then draw your own conclusions, make your own judgments and decide what you believe.

ENDNOTES

The quotation from Albert Einstein at the beginning of this book
is from an Internet newsletter.

1. Davis, Wade, *Shadows in the Sun*, p. 8.

2. Joy, Brugh, *Avalanche*, p. 224.

3. Moyne, John, and Coleman Barks, *Unseen Rain*, p. 65.

4. Quoted in "Babylon 5," in January 1995.

5. King, Serge, *Earth Energies*, p. 177.

FURTHER READING

Abadin, M.J. *Your Psychic Potential.* Adams Media Corporation, Holbrook, Massachusetts, 1995

Davis, Wade. *Shadows in the Sun: Essays on the Spirit of Place.* Lone Pine Publishing, Edmonton, Alberta, 1992

Devereux, Paul. *Shamanism and the Mystery Lines: Ley Lines, Spirit Paths, Shape-Shifting and Out-of-Body Travel.* Llewellyn Publishers, St. Paul, Minnesota, 1993

Gell-Mann, Murray. *The Quark and the Jaguar: Adventures in the Simple and the Complex.* W.H. Freeman and Company, New York City, New York, 1994

Greenwood, Dr. Michael, and Peter Nunn, M.D. *Paradox and Healing: A Book about Medicine, Mythology and Transformation.* PARADOX Publishers, Victoria, British Columbia, 1994

Hill, Beth. *Moonrakers.* Horsdal & Schubart Publishers Ltd., Victoria, British Columbia, 1997

Holzer, Hans. *Are You Psychic? Unlocking the Power Within.* Avery Publishing Group, New York City, New York, 1997

Joy, Brugh. *Avalanche: Heretical Reflections on the Dark and the Light.* Random House, New York City, New York, 1997

King, Serge. *Earth Energies: A Quest for the Hidden Power of the Planet.* Quest Books, Wheaton, Illinois, 1992

Kryder, Rowena Pattee. *Sacred Ground to Sacred Space: Visionary Ecology, Perennial Wisdom, Environmental Art and Ritual.* Bear & Company, Inc., Santa Fe, New Mexico, 1994

Moyne, John, and Coleman Barks. *Unseen Rain: Quatrains of Rumi.* Threshold Books, Putney, Vermont, 1986

Nicholson, Shirley, and Brenda Rosen. *Gaia's Hidden Life: The Unseen Intelligence of Nature.* The Theosophical Publishing House, Wheaton, Illinois, 1992

Noble, Vicki. *Shakti Woman: Feeling our Fire, Healing Our World — The New Female Shamanism.* Harper San Francisco, San Francisco, California, 1991

Parker, K. Langloh, and Johanna Lambert. *Wise Women of the Dreamtime: Aboriginal Tales of the Ancestral Powers.* Inner Tradition International, Rochester, Vermont, 1993

Parry, Danaan, and Lila Forest. *The Earthsteward's Handbook.* Sunstone Publications, Cooperstown, New York, 1987

Shealy, C. Norman, M.D., Ph.D., and Caroline M. Myss, M.A. *The Creation of Health: The Emotional, Psychological and Spiritual Responses that Promote Health and Healing.* Stillpoint Publishing, Walpole, New Hampshire, 1988, 1993

Stein, Diane. *Stroking the Python: Women's Psychic Lives*. Llewellyn Publications, St. Paul, Minnesota, 1988

Swimme, Brian, and Thomas Berry. *The Universe Story: From the Primordial Flaring Forth to the Ecozoic Era — A Celebration of the Unfolding of the Cosmos*. HarperCollins, New York City, New York, 1992